A CULTURALLY RESPONSIVE APPROACH

Using
WebQuests
in the
Social Studies
Classroom

Margaret M. Thombs • Maureen M. Gillis • Alan S. Canestrari

CORWIN PRESS
A SAGE Company
Thousand Oaks, CA 91320

For information:

Corwin Press
A SAGE Company
2455 Teller Road
Thousand Oaks, California 91320
www.corwinpress.com

SAGE Publications Ltd.
1 Oliver's Yard
55 City Road
London, EC1Y 1SP
United Kingdom

SAGE Publications India Pvt. Ltd.
B 1/I 1 Mohan Cooperative
Industrial Area
Mathura Road, New Delhi 110 044
India

SAGE Publications Asia-Pacific Pte. Ltd.
33 Pekin Street #02-01
Far East Square
Singapore 048763

Printed in the United States of America.

Library of Congress Cataloging-in-Publication Data

Thombs, Margaret M.
  Using webquests in the social studies classroom : a culturally
responsive approach / Margaret M. Thombs, Maureen M. Gillis, Alan S. Canestrari.
      p. cm.
  Includes bibliographical references and index.
  ISBN 978-1-4129-5950-6 (cloth : acid-free paper) — ISBN
978-1-4129-5951-3 (pbk. : acid-free paper)
  1. Social sciences—Problems, exercises, etc. 2. Social
sciences—Study and teaching—Activity programs. 3. Internet—Activity
programs. 4. Activity programs in education. 5. Internet—Study and
teaching. 6. Education—Computer network resources. 7.
Teaching—Computer network resources. 8. Internet in education. I.
Gillis, Maureen M. II. Canestrari, Alan S. III. Title.
  H62.3.T46 2009
  300.78'5—dc22
                                    2008004862

This book is printed on acid-free paper.

08 09 10 11 10 9 8 7 6 5 4 3 2 1

Acquisitions Editor: Cathy Hernandez
Editorial Assistants: Megan Bedell and Ena Rosen
Production Editor: Appingo Publishing Services
Cover Designer: Lisa Riley

Contents

Preface

*U*sing WebQuests in the Social Studies Classroom: A Culturally Responsive Approach* provides a practical approach for using WebQuests in the secondary social studies classroom. It helps teachers respond to three important questions facing them today:

> How can I be a more culturally responsive teacher?
> How can I help make social studies engaging for my students?
> How might technology facilitate my work and that of my students?

WHY THIS BOOK?

Today's classroom is more culturally rich than ever before, and new technology tools emerge so fast that often our students are more conversant with "the latest gizmos" than we are. So how do we engage this young, diverse group in subjects they might feel are dry and meaningless? How do we make the social sciences personal and real, so that students embrace the learning needed to help them become good, global citizens?

Our focus is on how teachers can optimize learning, enhance student inquiry, and promote greater intercultural understanding by infusing a simple, yet powerful, technology into their daily classroom work. In the traditional secondary classroom, lessons tend to start, on any given day, from where the lecture left off the previous day. This text provides instruction for using a proven technology and process (the WebQuest) to transport students from the present to the past and back, in and out of personal and cultural connections to history and other social sciences, in order to connect learners directly with curriculum content.

WebQuests are inquiry-oriented, collaborative activities that focus on using Web-based information to enhance higher-level analysis, synthesis, and evaluation. WebQuest assignments pose a stimulating and genuine problem for students to solve; direct them to resources that will provide up-to-date information and provoke analysis; and culminate in achievable, measurable results. Many teachers and educational programs worldwide have adopted this award-winning model for every type of primary- and secondary-level course. A number of scholarly articles in various trade publications describe the WebQuest methodology, but no comprehensive resource exists to provide professional development for teachers who want to develop a variety of models for use during an entire semester of coursework for a specific curriculum.

This book incorporates professional reflection and guided practice tools to facilitate such professional development. Using actual student stories inserted into vignettes that portray typical, culturally diverse classrooms, each chapter walks you through a series of exercises that will help you begin to answer the three important questions previously asked. We intend to enhance, not duplicate, the extensive resources available online for creating WebQuests by incorporating social studies topics (specifically, culturally responsive topics) and using a reflective approach with exercises based on the vignettes.

The first few chapters address today's culturally diverse classroom, the latest technology standards focusing on required skills, and the history and general process for creating WebQuests. Then, each chapter describes how to develop specific WebQuest components by using actual student voices and typical classroom challenges in a series of exercises throughout each module. Comprehensive examples of culturally responsive WebQuests used in the exercises throughout the book are included in five of the chapters.

Teaching cultural sensitivity is important—perhaps more so—even if your classroom is not diverse. And even though the vignettes and exercises in this text focus on experiences of more recent immigrants, the lessons you develop using this approach can just as easily integrate the cultural backgrounds of students from Native American, African American, or more traditional Western European heritages.

REAL VOICES . . .
TYPICAL CLASSROOM CHALLENGES

Soso, a native of Zambia, looks to his father to teach him about his country and cultural background via the Internet "because we really don't do much of that at all in school." How can Frank Parker, Soso's tenth-grade history teacher, engage his diverse class and make the study of history, economics, health, and sociology personal? How can he use technology to focus on complex problem solving to guide these students in civically responsible decision making?

Anita Bertz has never been satisfied with her lesson plan about world religions. Anita's world history classroom this year includes Happy-Hardy Guinguing, an ESL student from the Philippines. When given the chance to write about his country and culture, he states, "Thank you for listening to what I have to say. I never express myself like this before. I feel less to be ashamed." Can Anita create a WebQuest that will encourage students like Happy-Hardy to express themselves in ways they never have while gaining a deeper understanding of the root causes of religious conflict?

Juan from Maria Borden's social studies class tells about his first experiences as a young student whose father had brought his family to America from Mexico. Trying to learn in the classroom without understanding the language was so exhausting, he would sleep from the time he got home from school until the next morning. Now he is more fluent in English but finds his courses are too American-centric; he wishes his classmates had more opportunities to learn about his country and his culture. How does Maria handle the challenge of teaching about American immigration to a classroom where the experience might be personal—and painful?

Ron Kowal wants to use technology in his sophomore geography class to engage his students. Vladi is from Bulgaria and Russia and loves to share his knowledge of Eastern Europe with others. What technologies can Mr. Kowal introduce to his class to transform mapping from paper and globes to a more interactive, creative, and exciting assignment? How can he integrate experiences and enthusiasm like Vladi's into this lesson?

Jared Zawod believed his student Haseena's quiet nature was due to shyness or language difficulty and was surprised—and disappointed in himself—when he learned that her culture's respect for authority drove her subdued classroom behavior. The experience made him realize that his civics lesson plan on voting rights and responsibilities had become rote. Now that he understands more about his Afghan student, he finds a way to breathe new life into his curriculum.

Poroma is a student from Bangladesh who finds her American teachers somewhat unapproachable. Her sociology teacher, Janeka Gonzales, decides to use Bangladesh's recent history to go beyond textbook discourses on the social impacts of industrialization of agrarian economies. Can she make Poroma feel more included while creating a real and relevant lesson for her class?

Do you have students like Soso, Happy-Hardy, Juan, Vladi, Haseena, and Poroma in your classroom? Or is your classroom less diverse, but you want to create a more global and inclusive atmosphere to help your students become better world citizens?

PRACTICAL, USABLE CURRICULUM CONTENT

Using these classroom examples, each chapter employs a workbook approach to stimulate thinking about how to integrate cultural responsiveness and technology to engage your students in your particular curriculum. Five completed, culturally responsive social studies WebQuests are included as examples, and instructions reference the National Council for Social Studies Standards (NCSS) strands, the American Historical Association's criteria for Excellent Classroom Teaching, and the International Society for Technology in Education (ISTE) standards into all modules.

This text is intended for coursework in secondary history/social studies methodology and classroom applications of technology courses on both undergraduate and graduate levels. It will also be useful as a guide for professional development workshops and seminars for teachers interested in learning more about engaging culturally responsive social studies and technologically enhanced instruction. And current practitioners who might not be taking a course on these topics will find that the workbook format facilitates self-study. Implementing the methodology in this guide is a step toward infusing humanistic education into the classroom.

Acknowledgments

We want to thank the professionals at Corwin Press, particularly Acquisitions Editor Cathy Hernandez, Associate Editor Megan Bedell, Editorial Assistant Ena Rosen, and the production services of Belinda Thresher and Appingo, whose assistance throughout this process was invaluable.

Without Bernie Dodge and Tom March, we would not have WebQuests and all its powerful support tools to use in our classrooms. We extend our thanks and admiration to them for their dedication to students and teachers and for sharing their technology, time, and effort so freely.

Students Harrison (Soso) Songolo, Happy-Hardy Guinguing, Juan Pablo Escoriza, Vladimir (Vladi) Emilov Evtimov, Haseena Niazi, and Poroma Kanya generously shared their personal stories with us and helped make this book real. In addition, colleagues Luis Oliveira and Bruce Marlowe gave us the benefit of their experiences teaching in culturally diverse classrooms. Thank you!

PUBLISHER'S ACKNOWLEDGMENTS

Corwin Press gratefully acknowledges the contributions of the following reviewers:

Carrie Ames
Social Studies Teacher
Gallup High School
Gallup, MN

Kevin Brandon
Social Studies Teacher
Los Angeles Unified School District
Los Angeles, CA

Dean Antonio Cantu
Professor and Dean of Education
Indiana University Kokomo
Kokomo, IN

Michael F. Crull
Principal
West Jay Middle School
Dunkirk, IN

Amy Davies
Social Studies Teacher
Taylor Alderdice High School
Greensburg, PA

Toni DeKiere-Phillips
Social Studies and Special Education Teacher
Stockbridge High School
Stockbridge, GA

Susan Gogue
Social Studies Teacher
Jack Young Middle School
Baraboo, WI

Denise Mullen
Social Studies Teacher
James Monroe Middle School
Albuquerque, NM

Greg Oppel
Social Studies Teacher
Edmond Memorial High School
Edmond, OK

Shawn White
Social Studies Teacher
Weston McEwen High School
Milton Freewater, OR

Marian White-Hood
Director of Academics, Accountability, and Principal Support
Maya Angelou Public Charter Schools and the See Forever Foundation
Washington, DC

About the Authors

Margaret M. Thombs is an associate professor of education specializing in instructional technology at Roger Williams University in Bristol, Rhode Island. She earned her PhD in computing technology in education from Nova Southeastern University. She has taught secondary mathematics and computer science and was formerly the director of technology for the Middletown, Rhode Island, Public Schools. Her areas of expertise include facilitating English as a second language skills using technology and technology-enabled family and local history research. She is a frequent presenter at national and regional technology and education conferences and has authored a number of articles on technology integration in the classroom. She and her family live in Rhode Island.

Maureen M. Gillis is the owner of an Internet-based business and the coordinating editor for Spalding University's manuscript review program for MFA alumni in Louisville, Kentucky. She earned her MFA in writing from Spalding and has taught in that program. Prior to becoming a writer and Internet entrepreneur, she was a CPA and business executive and taught in the MBA program at the University of Hartford. She serves as the writing coach for the management team of the Connecticut Coalition Against Domestic Violence. Maureen and her husband live in Connecticut.

Alan S. Canestrari is the editor (with Bruce Marlowe) of *Educational Foundations: An Anthology of Critical Readings* (Sage 2004), which received the 2005 American Education Studies Critics' Choice book award, and *Educational Psychology in Context: Readings for Future Teachers* (Sage 2006). In addition, Alan has contributed to *Integrating Inquiry Across the Curriculum* (Corwin Press 2005) by Richard Audet and Linda Jordan. The journal *Encounter: Education for Meaning and Social Justice* published "From Silence to Dissent: Fostering Critical Voice in Teachers" (Winter 2005). He earned his EdD from Boston University. Alan has had a long career as a social studies teacher, department chair, and history educator. He was named Rhode Island Teacher of the Year in 1992. He and his family live in Barrington, Rhode Island.

1 The Challenge of Culturally Responsive Teaching

MEET HARRISON SONGOLO . . .

My friends call me Soso. I was born in Zambia in a city called Flura in an area called Kitwe. That's where a lot of Bemba people are from. I lived with my grandparents, their kids, and my mother and me all together. But now I live here in the United States with just my mother and father. In Zambia, I went to school on a bus, not like a school bus but a city bus. Here I take the school bus. I like going to the high school. It's really big and I get lost sometimes. I am in the tenth grade and I really have good teachers. They are a little bit strict but I can tell that they are going to be helpful. My English teacher is pretty interested in my background, my culture. Everybody in the class wrote an autobiography so I wrote about my life back in Zambia, mostly about family and friends. She was pretty surprised and she liked it a lot too.

My life here and back in Zambia is completely different. Here we have television. We also have television over in Zambia but not as many channels. But usually I spent most of my time playing outside with a bunch of friends of mine. During a certain season when the mangoes grow, we'd go in the trees, spend the whole day just eating mangoes. Sometimes we'd play soccer and other games. In history class when we talked about nations, the teacher asked each one of us about our backgrounds and I just mentioned things about Zambia. My dad, who just became naturalized, has kind of shown me more things about Zambia and my cultural background using the Internet but we really don't do much of that at all in school.

Soso is enrolled in Frank Parker's tenth-grade history class this year. Mr. Parker is looking for ways to motivate Soso and his other students, who make a diverse group. He knows that classrooms across the nation are becoming less homogeneous each day. Curious to know whether his classroom is typical of others across the country, Frank recently consulted the U. S. Department of Education's National Center for Education Statistics Web site. What he found in viewing their Fast Facts tab and searching their articles did not surprise him; the importance of responding to immigrant students and students whose primary language is not English is supported by a number of important statistics.

- In 2005, 42% of public school students belonged to a racial or ethnic minority group, which is an increase from 22% of students in 1972 (2007b).
- For the 2003–2004 school year, 11% of students received English as a second language (ESL) services. California was the highest at 26%, followed by Texas at 16% (2006).
- Between 1979 and 2005, the number of school-age children (ages 5 to 17) who spoke a language other than English at home increased from 3.8 million to 10.6 million (2007a).

From 1972 to 2005, the number of students considered a racial or ethnic minority has nearly doubled. Figure 1.1 describes minority enrollment in public schools for grades K–12. For information on demographics and statistics for your region, consult http://nces.ed.gov/.

Statistics sometimes discourage Frank Parker. Various commissions and organizations continue to report increases in the rates of failing schools and failing children. What motivates Frank, however, is not so much the at-risk rhetoric but real children like Soso who have real needs—the kids he works with every day.

Frank Parker is a great teacher. He, like many of his colleagues, is competent and caring; his students can count on him to provide a secure and challenging learning environment. One characteristic that sets him apart from many of his colleagues, however, is his initiative—particularly

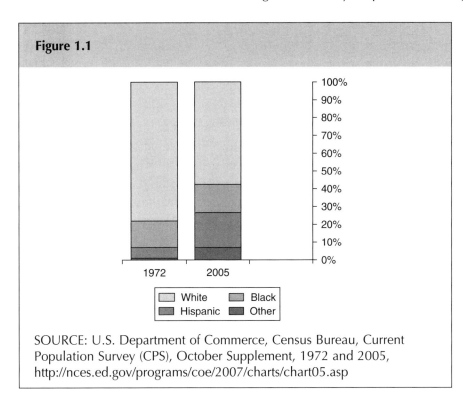

Figure 1.1

SOURCE: U.S. Department of Commerce, Census Bureau, Current Population Survey (CPS), October Supplement, 1972 and 2005, http://nces.ed.gov/programs/coe/2007/charts/chart05.asp

when it comes to professional development. Frank is not content waiting for districtwide workshops, especially when he perceives an immediate need. He is impatient. He knows that Soso, like his other students, needs his attention now.

Earlier today, when Frank visited the school before the beginning of the fall term, he stopped at the main office to pick up his course rosters. As he read the names Robert Alipala, Elsa Chang, Diego Garza, Carrie Meeks, Antonio Silva, and Harrison Songolo, he thought about how he could engage this group of learners. *How can I be a more culturally responsive teacher? How can I help make history compelling for them? And how might technology facilitate my work and that of the students?*

How you would respond to Mr. Parker's questions?

THE NEED FOR A CULTURALLY RESPONSIVE CONTEXT

All teaching is contextual. Powerful, *culturally responsive* pedagogy requires that curricula and instructional frameworks be based, at least in part, on students' actual experiences. Students of different cultural groups might encounter teachers who have "culturally blind" attitudes, teachers who teach under the "fallacy of homogeneity," or instructors who have preconceived notions, however innocent, about them and their culture. Or if they are lucky, they are assigned teachers who have concluded that teaching is "most effective when ecological factors, such as prior experiences, community settings, cultural backgrounds, and ethnic identities of teachers and students are included in its implementation" (Gay, 2000, p. 4). Unfortunately, not all teachers engage students in this way.

Mr. Parker (and you) might begin by reflecting on his (and your) teaching practices by asking the following questions, adapted from a discussion of culturally responsive characteristics in *Culturally Responsive Teaching* by Geneva Gay (2000, pp. 29–36).

- In what ways is my teaching **validating**? How am I using the cultural knowledge, prior experiences, frames of reference, and performance styles of diverse students to make learning encounters more relevant and effective for them?
- In what ways is my teaching **comprehensive**? Am I using instructional approaches to help students maintain identity and connections with their ethnic groups and communities? How do I encourage them to develop a sense of community, friendship, and shared responsibility . . . to acquire an ethic of success? Are expectations and skills interwoven throughout the curriculum? Does my instruction help them internalize the value of learning as communal, reciprocal, and interdependent?
- In what ways is my teaching **multidimensional**? How can I better collaborate on content, learning contexts, classroom climate, student–teacher relationships, instructional techniques, and performance assessments in order to provide a more integrated and interdisciplinary experience for the students?

- In what ways is my teaching **empowering**? Do I enable students to become academically competent and confident? Is my instruction participatory, problem based, dialogic, active, and inquiring?
- In what ways is my teaching **transformative**? How do I guide students in developing the knowledge, skills, and values needed to become social activists?
- In what ways is my teaching **emancipatory**? How can I encourage students to find their voices, to contextualize issues in multiple cultural perspectives, to engage in multiple ways of knowing and thinking? Do I help them become more active participants in shaping their learning?

It is a lot to think about. So what might our first step to transform instruction be? How might we extend our thoughts concerning Gay's (2000) questions and link them to the larger narrative?

The Larger Narrative

"Dead head" history, unfortunately, is alive and well in our classrooms. Students in these classes are often taught using a "heroes and holidays" or "additive" approach to teaching (Banks, 2001). This perspective reinforces the notion that history is remote from students' personal experiences and therefore disconnected from their lives. More disquietingly, it teaches—in both subtle and explicit ways—that white, western history is at the center of how civilizations have unfolded, and everything else (though sometimes interesting and exotic) is extraneous and unimportant to *real* history. Unsurprisingly, when students feel excluded from their own history, they find it boring and useless. Further, instruction based on virtually all textbooks hinders students' capacity to see diversity—or themselves, for that matter—in history. Rather, teachers must cultivate a classroom community of learners, a classroom that embraces and affirms diversity (Ladson-Billings, 2001; Nieto, 1999, 2000). They must actively engage students and help them construct knowledge through inquiry and attach meaning to that knowledge through dialogue (Villegas & Lucas, 2002). The classroom must be based upon a vision of pluralism, participatory democracy, and relevancy where students make correlations with their own personal experience and histories (Barton & Levstik, 2004). So how can teachers activate students' interest in history given these notions? How can teachers connect students to the larger narrative in which they and their ancestors play a role?

We suggest that teachers might begin to think about their students as qualitative researchers—ethnographers of sorts—involved in activities that locate them as not just observers but, more importantly, as participants in the world. Students then become part of the "historical moment," engaging in "critical conversations about democracy, race, gender, class, nation-states, globalization, freedom, and community" (Denzin & Lincoln, 2000, pp. 2–3). If they are able to place themselves and their families *within* specific historical events, their understanding of the world falls into a meaningful context. Students then perceive history as situated in accounts, descriptions, interpretations, and representations of people rather than simply of events. How do we begin to position students as historical actors, as people with real voices who can identify and connect with history?

Powerful Social Studies . . . Powerful Citizens

We can begin by thinking about our purpose as history teachers and social scientists. Our work should be "grounded in a single, overarching purpose— preparation for participatory, pluralist democracy" (Barton & Levstik, 2004, p. 20). To achieve this, social sciences teachers need to engage their students in powerful teaching and learning. This notion is discussed extensively in the National Council for the Social Studies' (1992) position statement, *A Vision of Powerful Teaching and Learning in the Social Studies: Building Social Understanding and Civic Efficacy.* The statement reaffirms "citizen education as the primary purpose of social studies" (p. 157) and suggests that this purpose can be achieved through teaching and learning that is "meaningful, integrative, value-based, challenging, and active" (p. 162). Like Frank Parker, we can begin with powerful social studies teaching and learning based upon our concern for the common good and the idea that citizen participation in public life is essential to the health of our democratic system. What experiences, then, should our social studies programs provide?

Teachers today use standards to inform their practice. Standards can be helpful, but teachers must be careful not to miss the point. For example, posting standards around the classroom does little to improve teaching and learning or to guarantee student achievement. Even citing standards as goal statements might add little to building social understanding and civic efficacy.

We believe the NCSS standards should serve as a guide rather than a rigid scope and sequence prescription. Think of them as conveying *how* ideas could be taught rather than *what* ideas should be taught. For example, look at the following strand and indicator and write down your ideas about how instruction might help Soso and his classmates meet the standard. (See Other Resources: A located in the back of this book to examine NCSS's ten thematic strands.)

II. Time, Continuity, and Change

Social studies programs should include experiences that provide for the study of the *ways human beings view themselves in and over time,* so that the learner can:

e. investigate, interpret, and analyze multiple historical and contemporary viewpoints within and across cultures related to important events, recurring dilemmas, and persistent issues, while employing empathy, skepticism, and critical judgment.

What do you think?

_____

_____

_____

_____

Challenging? Of course. Engaging students in powerful teaching and learning is exceedingly complex. Where should Mr. Parker (and we) start, especially with students like Soso and his classmates, who may never have been engaged in this way before?

IMAGINATIVE ENTRY

We believe that powerful social studies programs are grounded, in part, in "imaginative entry" (Barton & Levstik, 2004, p. 26). In the traditional classroom, on any given day, instruction tends to start from where the lecture left off on the previous day. Little effort is made to intentionally "scaffold inquiry to distant times and places" (p. 60). But teachers can use a number of tools to *zoom* students from the present to the past and back. "Imaginative entry" could include the following:

- *Connecting contemporary issues and events to the past.* For example, students might compare and contrast details about Hurricane Katrina and its aftermath with accounts of the Great San Francisco Earthquake of 1907.
- *Reading great nonfiction.* For example, students could extend their understanding of the complexities of the adolescent stage by reading *Coming of Age in Samoa* by Margaret Mead.

- *Reading great fiction.* For example, students might gain further insights into eleventh-century Japan by reading about pilgrimages to the Ishiyama-dera temple in *Tales of Genji* by Murasaki Shikibu.
- *Interpreting historical and other documents.* For example, students could read George F. Kennan's *Sources of Soviet Containment* to build a primary source foundation for understanding the Cold War.
- *Examining maps.* For example, exploring population distribution and vegetation maps of India could stimulate an analysis of the proximity of humans to animal habitats.

Think about the content of your curriculum. Choose a concept, theme, era, or event. What might be some of your own points of imaginative entry? Be inventive.

_____

_____

_____

_____

To extend these points, think about how you and your students might explore the four principal "stances" or historical perspectives offered by Barton and Levstik (2004) in *Teaching History for the Common Good.* These stances provide a useful model for engaging students in a purposeful way— a "doing" history way (p. 7). Doing history requires active teaching and learning. Teachers must plan activities that help students (1) *identify* or make connections between themselves and the past; (2) *analyze* or engage in historical thinking to explain causes and effect, for example; (3) *respond morally* or make judgments about events of the past; and (4) *exhibit* or display what they have discovered about the past (pp. 45–128).

The Quest for Connections

Take a moment to look back at the interview with Soso. What hints does the interview provide us about connecting Harrison Songolo to the history (or geography, sociology, politics, economy, anthropology, etc.) of the world? How might the four principal stances inform Soso and other students about "doing history"?

Hint	Identification	Analysis	Moral Response	Exhibition

How might guiding students to make personal connections encourage them to take responsibility for their own learning? How might, for example, analyzing primary source documents help students think and act like social scientists? How might an opportunity to make moral judgments help students think critically about issues facing the world? How might helping students demonstrate their understandings in creative and exciting ways make learning more engaging, evocative, and enduring?

As we have previously indicated, there are many ways to engage students constructively within the historical and sociopolitical context of multiculturalism. Our intention here, however, is to limit our discussion of a single, detailed imaginative entry—the WebQuest—as a way to provide social studies teachers with an approach to connecting students' personal narratives to the larger social narrative. As discussed in detail in the following chapters, WebQuests are inquiry-oriented, collaborative assignments that focus on using Web-based information to enhance higher-level analysis, synthesis, and evaluation. Activities are designed to pose authentic, motivating problems, to direct students to resources that provoke analysis, and to culminate in an achievable, measurable result.

Why technology? Why WebQuests? Chapter 2 features a review of what technologically literate teachers and students ought to know, and Chapters 3 and 4 introduce the WebQuest as a source of rich historical, cultural, and genealogical information.

2 The Technologically Competent Social Studies Teacher

F rank Parker, our social studies teacher from Chapter 1, teaches in a large urban school district. Frank considers himself proficient in the personal use of technology but wonders how he could do a better job infusing technology into his curriculum. He has two computers in his classroom, one of which is five years old. He can also sign up to use a computer lab that has twenty-four Internet-connected computers. Although familiar with the software on these computers, he wonders if there are social studies-specific technology resources that might benefit his students.

When technology was first introduced into the classroom in the late 1970s, few teachers envisioned its impact on their professional lives. In the span of thirty years, we have seen exponential growth in the quantity and quality of available resources. This development, however, has brought challenges as well as benefits. Today, teachers like Frank Parker are expected to be not only proficient with the personal use of technology, but also adept at curriculum integration.

What are the skills and conditions needed to create a technology-rich environment in the social studies classroom? How can Frank Parker become competent and confident with respect to technology integration? How can technology serve the needs of his diverse learners? To answer these questions, we need to look at national technology standards for students and examine how teachers can help them meet these standards in the social studies classroom.

THE NETS PROJECT

In 1998, the International Society for Technology in Education (ISTE) released the National Education Technology Standards for Students (NETS–S). Six standards described what K–12 students should know and what they should be able to do with respect to technology. In June 2007, ISTE released the next generation of student standards. The revised standards focus less on tools and more on skills. The six standards are as follows: Creativity and Innovation; Communication and Collaboration; Research and Information Fluency; Critical Thinking, Problem Solving, and Decision Making; Digital Citizenship; and Technology Operations and Concepts. The full text of the standards is included in Other Resources: B located at the back of this book. (Note that in 2000, ISTE issued Standards for Teachers [NETS-T] that supported the student standards and plans to update these to parallel the new standards. By the time this book is published, NETS-T should be available; check ISTE's Web site at http://www.iste.org/.)

Producing technologically competent students requires equally competent teachers. After examining the details of student standards in Other Resources: B, what additional technology training do you consider a priority for your professional development in the next twelve months? within the next two years?

ESSENTIAL CONDITIONS FOR SUCCESSFUL TECHNOLOGY INTEGRATION

The lack of technology resources and support in his school often frustrates Frank Parker. He wants his students to have the same advantages that students in nearby suburban districts have. Since many of his students do not have computers at home, he considers it even more critical to procure additional resources and training for them.

ISTE has determined a number of essential conditions that need to be in place for teachers like Frank to be effective when integrating technology. What can teachers expect from their administrators and their school districts? How can a teacher design his or her own professional development experiences so that technology is used in powerful ways to engage students? Among these identified conditions are

- a proactive leadership that provides both vision and support;
- skilled educators who have access to appropriate professional development;
- access to up-to-date technology resources;
- a learning environment that is student-centered; and
- adequate support in terms of expertise and financial resources.

As you examine the resources and conditions in your school, are there any gaps you can identify that must be filled before the essential conditions are in place?

_____

_____

_____

What other items would you put on your technology "wish list"?

_____

_____

_____

TECHNOLOGY RESOURCES

Frank Parker sees potential for technology to engage his social studies students in exciting ways while addressing the NCSS thematic strands in a culturally responsive manner. Extensive Internet resources give his students access to online historical documents and other primary source materials, cultural resources, and interactive maps. Frank imagines collaborating with teachers and students from around the world, adding an electrifying new dimension to the social studies curriculum.

In addition to online resources, other technology tools offer the potential to engage students in constructive and stimulating learning activities. We will suggest many of these in the following chapters. To brainstorm potential uses for classroom technology, Frank wrote down his ideas for using the resources available in his school as he planned social studies lessons. He first considered ways to use desktop publishing software and decided that he could have his students

- create reports that communicate the culture and resources of places they are studying;
- act as Civil War reporters and produce a newspaper; or
- make posters to support their positions in a classroom debate.

Brainstorm ways you could use the following resources in your classroom.

Spreadsheets, including the ability to create charts and graphs (e.g., Excel)

_____

_____

_____

Image editing software or art programs

_____

_____

_____

Digital cameras and scanners

_____

_____

_____

Graphic organizer software tools (e.g., Inspiration®)

_____

_____

_____

Web page creation software

_____

_____

_____

Presentation software (e.g., PowerPoint)

_____

_____

_____

Digital video

_____

_____

_____

SPECIAL CONSIDERATIONS FOR CLASSROOM TECHNOLOGY

Web Site Accessibility

Mr. Parker wants to leverage as much technology as possible in his class-room and knows he must also meet the needs of students with physical or cognitive disabilities. When planning lessons, he wants to choose technology resources that encourage higher-level thinking and foster a constructivist environment. He wants to be certain that students like Soso and some of his classmates, whose primary language is not English, will benefit as much as their classmates will. Web sites used in the classroom must be analyzed for accessibility, content quality, and readability, but Frank is not sure how to accomplish this. Chapter 8 covers these issues and describes tools you can use to select appropriate Web sites. Meanwhile, if you are unfamiliar with general or Section 508 accessibility issues, refer to http://www.webaim.org/ and http://www.section508.gov/. Information on alternative Web browsing is found at http://www.w3.org/WAI/References/Browsing. Although this site has not been maintained in several years and several links to specified resources do not work, it contains the most comprehensive list of browsers and other tools, including screen readers and voice browsers, designed to enhance Web accessibility for all types of users that we can find.

Assistive Technology

In addition to analyzing the Web sites his students will access, Frank also needs to determine the effectiveness and usefulness of any technology used in his curriculum. He wants to make sure that available hardware, and the software programs he chooses, meet the needs of students with a range of ability levels and a variety of learning styles. To accomplish this, Frank consults the resource teachers for students with special needs. When selecting software, he looks for programs that are flexible with respect to difficulty levels, have captioning for spoken text, and are compatible with different types of input devices, such as joysticks and switches. Product information on assistive technology solutions is available at http://www.abilityhub.com/.

Legal Implications

Frank uses word processing, the Internet, and e-mail every day. He wonders what other ways technology might make his job easier. He wants to take advantage of as many resources as he can to develop professionally, but he sometimes does not know where to find the right tools. He is also concerned that he might not be aware of all legal implications affecting him and his students, such as Internet safety laws, copyright and fair use laws, and laws addressing students with special needs. Links to professional resources are found throughout the chapters of this book as they apply to a specific topic. For discussions on Internet safety, refer to http://www.isafe.org/ and http://www.netsmartz.org/educators.htm. Hall Davidson has information about copyright and fair use for the digital age at http://www.halldavidson.net/downloads.html. For special education laws, see http://www.wrightslaw.com/info/sec504.index.htm or http://www.504idea.org/504resources.html.

Online Technology Resources

The following are some additional technology resources designed specifically for educators:

- *eSchool News:* free electronic newsletter with technology news and product information for teachers, http://www .eschoolnews.com/
- *4teachers.org:* offers free online tools and resources to help teachers integrate technology into the classroom, http:// www.4teachers.org/
- *Teachers Using Technology:* technology discussion site (teachers can post questions; links to technology sites for teaching), http://www.teachersusingtechnology.com/
- *Google for Educators:* has classroom-specific search and technology tools, including a blog creator, free downloads for photo organization, 3-D modeling tool, and so forth, http://www.google.com/educators/index.html

---

Chapters 3 and 4 begin to examine the particularly engaging Web-based learning activity that is the focus of this book. We will look at the history of WebQuests, explain the standard components of the process, outline the design process, and present resources and tools available to assist you in creating WebQuests and implementing them into your curriculum. The remaining chapters, covering the detailed components of culturally responsive WebQuests in the social studies classroom, will integrate the technology concepts introduced in this chapter into a variety of exercises and lessons. The example WebQuests contained in this book are also mapped to the NCSS Social Studies Strands and to the 2007 NETS-S in Other Resources: D.

3 The WebQuest Model

While researching how to use technology to engage his students in a meaningful way, Frank Parker discovered that many schools around the world were using WebQuests. He had heard about them before, but he hadn't really thought about how that type of lesson could maximize technology—both for efficiency and for students' transformative learning—and also reach far beyond the textbooks for cultural responsiveness. WebQuests weren't a new concept, he learned, but the tools and ideas about how to use them were constantly improving.

BACKGROUND AND HISTORY

Bernie Dodge, professor of educational technology at San Diego State University, developed the WebQuest learning activity in 1995 as a means of integrating the most effective teaching methods into an efficient, technology-based process. Over the next several years, he and his colleague, educational designer Tom March, experimented with creating WebQuests that focused on motivating students and developing their critical thinking skills in a cooperative learning environment. Since then, this process has become a widely accepted, technology-based, problem-solving activity in classrooms throughout the world. In one measure of its popularity, Professor Dodge (2005) points out that his Internet search for the word "WebQuest" revealed more page hits than either "Kleenex" or "Clark Kent." Today, significant resources are available to help teachers create powerful WebQuests and leverage those built by others. And the primary criticism of WebQuests— that they are time-consuming to create—was addressed by Professor Dodge in late 2005 with the creation of QuestGarden, an online tool that guides the user through the design process and eliminates the need for Web editing skills. QuestGarden and other design tools are covered in the next chapter.

Ideally, WebQuest assignments pose a stimulating and genuine problem for students to solve; direct them to resources that will provide information and provoke analysis; and culminate in an achievable, measurable result. Initially conceived by Dodge (1995) as "an inquiry-oriented activity in which some or all of the information that learners interact with comes from resources on the internet" (¶ 2), the most effective WebQuests have evolved into classroom assignments that "not only involve some higher-level thinking, but require students to 'transform' what they have learned" (Dodge, 2005, ¶ 2).

Because so many online tools exist for building, assessing, and sharing WebQuests, this book is not intended to duplicate material readily available elsewhere. Our purpose is to provide a baseline understanding of the "why" and "how" of WebQuests, to communicate how this model can be used in the culturally responsive social studies classroom, and to guide you to other resources and tools that will facilitate the process of creating successful assignments.

WHY USE THE WEBQUEST MODEL?

In Chapter 1, we emphasized *imaginative entry*, a strategy that teachers might use to transport students from the present to the past and back or in and out of personal and cultural connections to the social sciences. WebQuests can be an ideal way to initiate imaginative entry. After the stage is set, students can engage in active role-playing, creative analysis, and real-world problem solving. History or geography becomes "about them" rather than disconnected facts about others.

Of course, cultural responsiveness and imaginative entry alone are not the only reasons to use this model. Other attributes accounting for its success in the classroom are as follows:

- *Flexibility*. WebQuests can be short term (designed to be completed in one to three classroom periods) or longer term (generally taking from one week to one month to complete). They can cover a single subject or integrate several disciplines, focus on a historical period or a thematic strand, and be used in an individual or team environment. For example, researching the relationships between medical advances and historical events can be an effective merging of science and social studies. Brainstorm other ways in which social studies and other disciplines can be combined, and list them on the following lines.

_____

_____

_____

_____

- *Focus on complex problem solving.* Links to primary source documents and other resources are provided in the assignment to make fact gathering efficient and reliable. The WebQuest uses a constructivist approach in which students move from the facts they research to formulation of ideas and solutions. Because the process incorporates the most effective instructional methods and resources are organized ahead of time, teachers can focus on listening to their students solve problems, rather than act as dispensers of facts. What kinds of real-world problems could you encourage your students to solve in your particular curriculum?

_____

_____

_____

_____

- *Motivating exercises.* Students access a wide range of current, relevant source documents in their quest to answer complex, yet meaningful, questions. The focus on authentic problems transforms assignments from hypothetical, classroom-only tasks to issues that students face in life. WebQuests encourage team problem solving; this dependency on others should result in motivated learning. Because students present their findings to peers, they want to excel.

What do you see as benefits and problems associated with working in groups?

_____

_____

_____

_____

- *Measurable results.* A rubric documents the outcomes against which students will be measured. The expected results can (and should) support NCSS and other standards. The rubric describes the performance criteria required to achieve proficiency across a scale from beginner level to exemplary. Describe how you currently use rubrics to assess your students' work.

_____

_____

_____

_____

- *Tools and support.* A number of sites, including Professor Dodge's, contain checklists, tutorials, example WebQuests, and other support and tools. The amount of Internet resources devoted to the WebQuest process is continuously expanding. Reference guides for many of these resources are provided throughout this book in the appropriate chapters.

EXAMPLE WEBQUEST NO. 1: EXPLORING SOCIOECONOMIC CONDITIONS

After learning more about WebQuests, Frank Parker reassessed his lesson plans while he thought about Soso and the rest of his students. He sat down at his computer and created an assignment that connected Soso's life experiences with lessons he wanted to teach about exploring current social, health, economic, and political conditions. Review his WebQuest (now shown) to become familiar with what a WebQuest looks like to a student. Chapter 4, which discusses the basics of designing WebQuests, will reference this example (as will the remaining chapters). We will examine components in more detail in Chapters 5 through 9, which contain additional example WebQuests.

WebQuest

One Zambia, One Nation?

▶ INTRODUCTION

For a substantial part of the 19th and 20th centuries, imperial powers, such as France, Belgium, Germany, Portugal, Spain, Italy, and Great Britain, controlled and exploited many African nations. After enslaving Africans, they conquered and colonized most of the continent. Intense rivalry existed among the conquerors, as they competed for territory, resources, and cultural dominance. The heat of the competition was cooled when the European powers met at the Berlin Conference in 1884 to "partition" (carve up) Africa. Africans fought back, but the Europeans were too strong and dominated affairs until after World War II. Then, Europe slowly gave way to freedom movements throughout the continent.

Today, Africa is still a place of great interest and much turmoil. We read about and see many disturbing images of tribal conflict, injustice, poverty, and disease. Zambia, like other modern African nations, did not always enjoy self-rule. What is happening in Zambia today and what does the future look like?

▶ TASK

In 1963, the British colony of Northern Rhodesia became Zambia. Above the reviewing stand at the formal independence ceremonies hung a very large and impressive banner that proclaimed, "One Zambia, One Nation." Is Zambia a unified nation? Has it made progress toward improved health care, a better standard of living for its people, peace between tribes, and democracy? You are part of a team of researchers for the World Health Organization

(WHO), and your task is to travel to Zambia to evaluate the social, political, economic, and health conditions there. When you return from your journey, you will present your analysis of Zambia's status and projections for the future to other members of WHO.

▶ Process

1. You will be assigned to one of six research teams. Each team will consist of *four* specialized researchers; you will be assigned to take on one of the following roles:
   ● Social expert—you will research social conditions such as employment and economic conditions.
   ● Health expert—you will research life expectancy, major health concerns, nutrition, and disease.
   ● Political expert—you will record the political environment of Zambia, including type of government, voting rights, and people currently in power.
   ● Economics expert—you will research the monetary unit, average wage, and number of people living in what is considered poverty.

2. Begin by determining the essential questions you need to research. For example, as a political expert, you might ask what the characteristics of a unified nation are. As a health expert, you might want to research the standards for appropriate health care. Record specific questions that will facilitate investigation in the area you have been assigned.

3. Use Inspiration® to create a graphic organizer that records your data collection.

4. Links to resources to find valid data to help you answer the questions you created are provided below.

5. Analyze your data. What are you discovering? For example, you might have found some data that shows that the Zambian government and health organizations have created educational programs to inform the people about the AIDS epidemic. What do you think about the programs' effectiveness? Form a hypothesis for what you consider the most important issue in your area of expertise.

6. Firm your hypothesis by finding additional data that supports your assumptions. Add this data to your organizer.

7. Your team will present your findings in an oral presentation supported by a PowerPoint presentation. Each expert must contribute three slides to the presentation. The first slide will present what you consider the most important issue. Include an image on this slide. The second slide will contain data represented in a graph or chart. The third slide will be a bulleted list of proposed solutions to the problem. Then, as a group, create Introductory and Summary slides to ensure a cohesive presentation. Your testimony should be persuasive and substantively supported by data. The use of maps, charts, and images will facilitate this.

8. As a group, present your evaluation to the other WHO teams and the Head of WHO (Mr. Parker). Each expert will present the slides he or she created. The first and last presenter will also review the Introduction or Summary slide, as appropriate. Be ready to respond to any questions WHO members ask.

▶ RESOURCES

Investigate the following:

1. https://www.cia.gov/library/publications/the-world-factbook/print/za.html
2. http://library.stanford.edu/africa/zambia.html
3. http://www.who.int/countries/zmb/en/
4. http://www.nationalgeographic.com/index.html/ (search Zambia)
5. Stay informed with http://www.time.com/ for daily Zambia news.
6. Roberts, A. (1976). *A History of Zambia.* Boston: Heinemann.
7. Kaunda, K. (1962). *Zambia Shall Be Free.* Boston: Heinemann.

▶ EVALUATION

The Head of WHO will evaluate your presentation using the following criteria:

1. Clarity of arguments presented
2. Quality of supporting data, maps, charts, and images
3. Persuasiveness of arguments
4. Overall quality of the presentation
5. Your research will be evaluated using your Inspiration® organizer

The following rubric will be used to assess your work.

	4	3	2	1
Statement of the Issue 20%	The issue is described clearly using specific data and examples.	The issue is described and facts are included, but not in sufficient detail.	The issue is described, but not supported by facts and details.	The issue is not described clearly.
Data 10%	The data presented supports the topic well. The graph represents the data in a clear and meaningful way.	The data presented supports the topic well. The graph represents the data but is not clear.	The data supports the topic, but is not complete. More data is needed.	The data does not support the topic.
Solutions 20%	The list of solutions contains four or more points. They relate to the problem well.	The list of solutions contains three points. They relate to the problem well.	The list of solutions contains two points. They relate to the problem well.	The list of solutions does not relate to the problem well.
Presentation 20%	The presentation was clear and professional. Questions were answered based on the research.	The presentation was clear and professional. Questions were answered based mostly on the research.	The presentation was clear and professional. Questions were answered based on opinion.	The presentation was unclear. Questions were not answered using the data.
Research 30%	The research is complete and the citations are correct. Four or more sources were used.	The research is complete and the citations are correct. Three sources were used.	The research is documented and the citations are correct. Less than three sources were used.	The research is not complete *or* sources were missing *or* not cited correctly.

▶ CONCLUSION

After all groups have presented, we will hold an open discussion of the essential questions. What do you think are the most pressing issues in Zambia today? Do you think similar issues exist in other African countries or in other parts of the world?

4 Designing WebQuests

O n his Web site *BestWebQuests.com,* Tom March (2007c) points out that many educators believe all Web-based lessons are WebQuests. True WebQuests, however, are designed for *problem-solving* activities related to well-defined learning objectives and follow a specific process and format. Before you learn how to build comprehensive and motivational WebQuests, it is important to become familiar with their core components: Introduction, Task, Process, and Evaluation. Keep in mind that we will delve into the finer points of each component in subsequent chapters.

CORE COMPONENTS OF A WEBQUEST

In this section, we will discuss the core components of a WebQuest by referring to "One Zambia, One Nation?" shown at the end of Chapter 3. This first culturally responsive example is a relatively short-term assignment that focuses on the NCSS thematic strands I, III, and VI. In this WebQuest, students explore and discuss aspects of the current and future landscape of Zambia, using the results of their research to create a presentation. This WebQuest, although it is a thought-provoking exercise, is relatively simple. As such, it was designed to help you begin to understand the core components and what differentiates an ideal WebQuest from a basic one. After reading about each component, we will ask you to consider what enhancements might be made to make the example assignment a more comprehensive and higher-level learning experience.

Introduction

The Introduction should perform two primary functions: give the students a clear indication of the topic they will be studying and create enthusiasm for the lesson. Reread the Introduction to "One Zambia, One Nation?"

Is the topic clearly identified? If not, how would you make it clearer?

_____

_____

_____

What aspects of this Introduction do you think will pique a student's interest? What would you add or change to make it more inviting?

_____

_____

_____

Task

The Task tells the students what they will do; it articulates the deliverable or end project. It is important that the Task be authentic (to employ higher-level thinking skills focused on real issues) and engaging (so that students are fully committed to the learning experience). Review the Task from "One Zambia, One Nation?"

Are the students asked to tackle a real and relevant problem? What improvements can make it more authentic?

_____

_____

_____

Would Frank's students (and yours) be excited about this assignment? Is the project challenging, yet achievable? What changes would you make, if any?

_____

_____

_____

Process

The Process section of the WebQuest describes how the assignment will be done (both individual and group work), provides links to the resources needed to complete the lesson, and gives the time frame for the work (in and outside the classroom).

What aspects of the Process are missing from "One Zambia, One Nation?"

_____

_____

_____

Choosing engaging and appropriate Web sites is critical in planning an effective WebQuest. Review the content of one of the Web sites Frank listed in his assignment. Is it appropriate for his tenth-grade history class? What features make the site engaging (or not)?

_____

_____

_____

What are some of the specific factors you would need to consider in selecting sites for _your_ class (e.g., assumed baseline knowledge, varying levels of proficiency in English, student reading levels, students with learning or other disabilities, etc.)?

_____

_____

_____

Brainstorm other types of Web sites Frank might have included to make the research process effective. Do not list specific sites, but rather categories or topics.

_____

_____

_____

Were the WebQuest instructions clear, for both how the group would work as a team and each role? Are there changes you would make?

_____

_____

_____

What other technology resources might Frank have used in his WebQuest?

_____

_____

_____

Evaluation

Evaluation of the students' final products is accomplished best by using rubrics. When students have access to the rubric as they complete the assignment, they should have clear expectations of what the assignment entails and can use the rubric for formative self-assessment. When you, as the teacher, evaluate the students' projects, rubrics make assessment equitable and organized.

For this WebQuest, Frank chose to use one rubric for the entire assignment. We will treat Evaluation in detail in Chapter 7; for now, can you identify any issues with Frank's rubric that might make it less effective for formative and summative assessment than it could be?

_____

_____

_____

Other Components of the Model

In addition to the core components already discussed, WebQuest pages usually contain a short conclusion and reference the source of any copyrighted images or text used with permission. Instructors usually include a Teacher Page to document the purpose of the lesson, the audience, resources, materials, and standards. Other instructors who want to use or adapt the WebQuest for their own classroom find this page helpful. Information on this page could include the following:

- a description of the genesis of the lesson and what it is about;
- the grade level and course (including curriculum standards) being addressed;
- details the teacher needs to know about the process (e.g., how the teams will be determined; how many class periods the lesson will take; and what materials, hardware, or software will be needed); and
- additional resources and links not already documented in the Process.

What would you include on a Teacher Page for "One Zambia, One Nation?"

_____

_____

_____

DESIGN PROCESS

In *Some Thoughts About WebQuests,* Bernie Dodge (1995) suggests,

> [L]earning to design WebQuests is a process that should go from the simple and familiar to the more complex and new. This means starting within a single discipline and a short-term WebQuest and then moving up to longer and more interdisciplinary activities. ("Design Steps," ¶ 1)

"One Zambia, One Nation?" is a good example of a teacher's first practice in developing these types of assignments.

Before you begin searching for Internet resources specific to your topics, you should familiarize yourself with the general resources available in your content area (primary source document and general information sites) and with WebQuest building tools. Many specific and general social studies and technology resources are listed in the textboxes called Online Resources in this and other chapters. Select a topic from your curriculum for which there are enough online resources for students to access, with a goal of encouraging higher-level problem-solving tasks. Document the NCSS standards and district standards or frameworks that will be met by investigating this topic. Select a design tool, and you are ready to begin.

Selecting a Primary Design Tool

Creating WebQuests can be accomplished in a number of ways. Web pages are written in a language called hypertext markup language (HTML), and some commonly used software products will produce HTML code for you with a simple "save as Web page" option. Many teachers use Microsoft Word or PowerPoint to create WebQuests because neither program requires additional software or technical training. Adding images and hyperlinks is achieved through the insert dropdown menu; students can directly access the Internet resources through the hyperlinks.

For teachers with some experience creating Web pages, an HTML editing program provides the opportunity to add special effects or configure multiple linked pages more easily. Many programs are available and range greatly in price. Web Weaver (McWeb Software), FrontPage (Microsoft), and Dreamweaver (Adobe) are three such products.

Publishing Web pages involves uploading the HTML code files to the school Web site server or another host server. This is not essential, unless you want students (or other teachers) to access the material from home or from a remote site. Storing the pages on the local school (vs. host) server allows students to access the pages in the classroom and link directly to Internet resources.

QuestGarden

In addition to the methods just described, the interactive, online tool QuestGarden is not just a resource for creating and storing WebQuests efficiently, but also provides a means of receiving feedback from other teachers on your product. You can design an assignment from scratch or adapt another WebQuest stored on the site. As of the date this book was published, QuestGarden offered a thirty-day, free trial period and charged a nominal $20 fee for a two-year subscription once the trial period expired. Bernie Dodge (1995) promises that new features will be added to the site over time.

Because QuestGarden provides an inexpensive, guided, and fully Web-enabled solution, the next five chapters, covering design elements in detail, will follow the order used by this tool, rather than the order in which the components are displayed in a completed WebQuest.

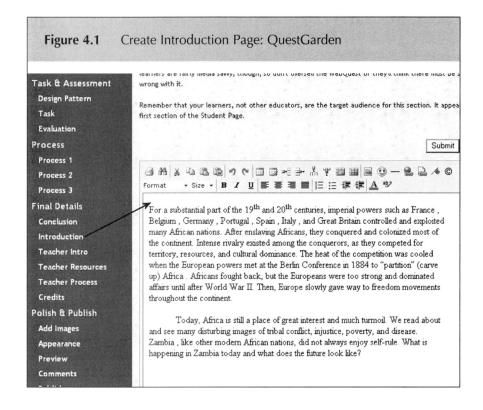

Figure 4.1   Create Introduction Page: QuestGarden

Figure 4.1 titled "Create Introduction Page: QuestGarden" is a screen shot of the Introduction created in this tool for the first example WebQuest contained in Chapter 3. Each of the headings on the left frame of the screen links to a guided page where you can create the particular component. In addition to walking you through inputting the core components and information for the Teacher Page, the tool makes it easy to add images and graphics and provides standard "design patterns" to follow.

ASSESSING WEBQUESTS

Once you have completed drafting your WebQuest, you can use the rubric on Tom March's (2007b) *ozline.com* to assess each component. This evaluation tool (located at http://bestwebquests.com/bwq/matrix.asp) scores your product from low to high for each of the following attributes: engaging introduction, task, background, roles, effective use of the Web, transformative thinking, real-world feedback, and your conclusion. After you assess your WebQuest, you can note any changes you wish to make and edit your assignment in the saved QuestGarden space.

Online Resources

Links to resources on the WebQuest design process are shown here. Review these sites before continuing on to the next chapter to become familiar with some of the resource materials and training available online.

SDSU College of Education and WebQuest.org

● The WebQuest Design Process—http://webquest.sdsu.edu/designsteps/index.html
● Useful WebQuest Resources—http://webquest.org/index-resources.php
● WebQuest Design Patterns—http://webquest.sdsu.edu/designpatterns/all.htm
● Adapting and Enhancing Existing WebQuests—http://webquest.sdsu.edu/adapting/index.html

Teachers First

● WebQuest Tutorial—http://www.teachersfirst.com/summer/webquest/quest-a.shtml

So let's get started!

5 Getting Started

Learners, Topics,
and Design Patterns

Absorbed in her notes, Anita Bertz almost missed her train stop. She was excited about creating a WebQuest for her tenth-grade students; the ideas discussed by the panel at the regional social studies conference were intriguing, and she knew the moderators had only enough time to outline the basics. The semester had just begun, and Anita had a range of topics to cover in her world history class. She glanced at the copy of the Tom March article a panelist had handed out. "Keep them Real, Rich, and Relevant," she read aloud. She had learned that the building blocks for good WebQuests were those that engaged students immediately, explored competing viewpoints, and asked questions that did not direct students to a single, "correct" answer.

What would engage *her* particular students? What would encourage them to reach outside themselves and their experiences but still be relevant to *them*? And where should she begin?

GETTING STARTED

As soon as she arrived home, Anita booted up her PC. Feeding the cat could wait! Before she began to think about what specific topics would be suitable WebQuests for her particular classroom, she decided to log on to WebQuest .org at http://webquest.org/index.php for help getting started. After spending a few minutes investigating some of the informational Web pages, she realized many of the lessons she wanted to cover in class could be enhanced by using the vast resources of the Internet to streamline data gathering so her students could focus on using analytical skills. She needed to select that type of assignment.

Before beginning your first WebQuest, take a few minutes to jot down your initial thoughts about choosing a topic. What portions of your lesson plan can make good use of the Web by providing students with links to most or all of the information they need to access so they can use their time applying analytic skills to focus on problem solving? Perhaps you have coursework with which you haven't been quite satisfied in the past and want to improve the outcomes. Or maybe textbook resources are inadequate or outdated.

_____

_____

_____

_____

_____

Anita's Classroom

Because Anita wanted to tailor her assignments to engage her diverse classroom, she knew she needed to understand more about each of her twenty-three students. She dug through her files and began reading the "Cultural Conversations" writing compilation that the ESL teacher had given her from the previous semester. Many of her current students had written about their countries, leisure time, and plans for the future. Because the community was a small, urban area on the outskirts of a city housing an international officers' school at a military college, almost 20 percent of her mainstreamed class was composed of children of matriculating officers from around the world. Two students were from the Asian Pacific area; one was from Brazil; and another was from Algeria. The remainder of the class was mostly third- or fourth-generation descendants of white, European immigrants.

As she read the essay one of her students had written, Anita tried to imagine how she would have felt if she had been a young girl living and learning in a non-English-speaking country. Would she have been so open about herself?

MEET HAPPY-HARDY GUINGUING . . .

The Philippines is over 7,000 islands with rich culture. The country symbolizes a lower average normal life. Almost all people of the Philippines are in turmoil. There are no jobs, making life for Filipinos seem hopeless. Some Filipinos are very smart. My brother Gentle is an example of a smart person. When he was very young, he read a lot of books, newspapers, dictionaries, and almost anything he can grab his hands on. He passes Middle school and High school like they were nothing. He was a College teacher but the College lost all its money and is now closed forever.

A few years ago, I was a kid who played video games for life. I was failing all my classes because I didn't want to do them. I blame myself for being stupid. I learn a lot of important things in my life. I listen to my parents and actually do what they told me to do. Now I play less video games and trying to do all my homework. I really like myself better because I don't do stupid things any more. Thank you for listening to what I have to say. I never express myself like this before. I feel less to be ashamed.

Anita knew one challenge in her class was the language barrier. She wanted to hold the tenth graders to high standards—they all had high potential—but not overwhelm them. As she read the essays, she concluded that most of her foreign students appreciated the opportunities the United States afforded them, while maintaining significant pride in their own countries. In some cases, though, they felt alienated despite believing that teenagers were "basically the same everywhere."

Who are your students (what grade and course are you writing a WebQuest to address)?

_____

_____

_____

What special challenges do your students face that you might want to consider in developing your WebQuest?

_____

_____

_____

BRAINSTORMING WEBQUEST IDEAS

General Social Studies

The National Council for the Social Studies Vision articulates five features of model social studies teaching and learning activities: lessons must be *meaningful, integrative, value-based, challenging,* and *active.* Ideas for WebQuest assignments should begin with these features in mind. A good place to start is by searching WebQuests that have already been reviewed for these attributes for the topics envisioned in your lesson plan for the semester.

- You can use keywords to search Tom March's *BestWebQuests.com* at http://bestwebquests.com/search.asp or review WebQuests sorted by subject and grade level at http://bestwebquests.com/. Note that the WebQuests referred to on this site are housed in many locations, and some of the links to the actual WebQuests are no longer working.

Other lists and examples of WebQuests that can be reviewed for leveraging are as follows:

- The QuestGarden search page at http://questgarden.com/search/index.php allows you to search by keyword, specific grade and curriculum area, or design pattern. Note that these WebQuests might be rated for quality, but many are not; they might contain useful information but are not necessarily examples of excellent WebQuests. However, because they are all housed in the QuestGarden site, you will be able to access all of them. You do not need to subscribe to QuestGarden to view any of the WebQuests on that site.
- The University of Richmond has compiled links to WebQuest projects, organized by study area and grade level, at http://oncampus.richmond.edu/academics/education/projects/. Again, some of these WebQuests might no longer be accessible.

Next, review your lesson plan for areas that lend themselves to collaborative activities designed for higher-level thinking skills (rather than memorization of facts). Are there areas you want to teach that would be enhanced by access to significant information not found in the standard texts? Are there primary source documents available on the Internet that you want your students to examine?

Online Resources: Social Studies Topics

The following sites might help you generate ideas for social studies topics:

National Council for the Social Studies (NCSS)

- Primary Site—http://www.socialstudies.org/
- NCSS Curriculum Standards for Social Studies Thematic Strands—http://www.socialstudies.org/standards/strands/

American Historical Association

- Statement on Excellent Classroom Teaching of History— http://www.historians.org/teaching/policy/ExcellentTeaching.htm

ERIC Digests

- Education Articles—http://www.ericdigests.org/

Pearson Education

- Social Studies Activities, Resources, and Events—http://www .sfsocialstudies.com/index2.html

SDSU College of Education

- Indices and Hotlists for Educators—http://edweb.sdsu.edu/ links/index.html

---

List four topics in your curriculum that might be good candidates for WebQuest assignments. Then determine the NCSS Thematic Strands (see Other Resources: A) that are addressed by these topics.

Topic	**Thematic Strand(s)**

1. _____

2. _____

3. _____

4. _____

Culturally Responsive Topics

Many books and papers have been written about culturally responsive teaching; this text is not intended as a primer on that subject. Culturally informed teaching is a lifelong learning process that requires multiple knowledge bases. Before attempting to create a culturally responsive WebQuest, a certain level of cultural competency is recommended. See Suggested Readings for books focused on culturally responsive teaching.

We suggested in Chapter 1 that teachers might think about their students as ethnographers; to do so, become an ethnographer yourself. First, understand your own culture and cultural biases; then, engage your students in conversations to help determine what assignments will be meaningful to them. A few ideas for culturally responsive activities that might be incorporated into a WebQuest are the following:

- using multicultural literature to study social class and power;
- interviewing students' families to develop oral histories of specific world events (historic or current);
- studying comparable events or circumstances in other countries to enhance understanding of U.S. history;
- analyzing ethnic art, poetry, or music vis-à-vis historical events to deepen knowledge of the cultural impact of such events; and
- investigating a range of cultural attitudes toward a similar frame of reference (e.g., family, education, health care, etc.)

Online Resources: Cultural Sensitivity

Here is a sample of some of the many online resources that might be helpful to you in creating assignments that are culturally responsive:

National Education Association

- Minority Community Outreach Articles—http://www.nea.org/mco/classroom.html

North Central Regional Educational Laboratory (Learning Point Associates)

- Various Articles on Multicultural Education (Type "multicultural" in the search box)—http://www.learningpt.org/

National Council of Teachers of English

● Ideas for Supporting Linguistically and Culturally Diverse Learners—http://www.ncte.org/groups/cee/positions/122892.htm

Multicultural Pavilion

● Multicultural Education Resources—http://www.edchange.org/multicultural/

New Horizons for Learning

● Links to Articles on Multicultural Education— http://www.newhorizons.org/strategies/multicultural/front_multicultural.htm

Eastern University (Pennsylvania)

● Electronic Magazine of Multicultural Education—http://eastern.edu/publications/emme/

Northern Arizona University

● Multicultural Education Internet Resource Guide—http://jan.ucc.nau.edu/~jar/Multi.html

ERIC Digest

● Culturally Responsive Teaching for American Indian Students Article—http://www.ericdigests.org/2005-1/teaching.htm

How can you meaningfully incorporate your students' specific cultural backgrounds into the four topics you listed earlier? Or are there other topics better suited to your class makeup? Keep in mind that cultural sensitivity not only is for the benefit of students from diverse backgrounds, but also is needed to broaden all students' knowledge and appreciation.

_____

_____

_____

_____

ANITA'S CHALLENGE:
TEACHING WORLD RELIGIONS

Anita has never been satisfied with her lesson plan on world religions. She feels that too much time is spent memorizing aspects of various religions rather than understanding the impact of religion and religious conflict on world cultures, particularly the economy and governmental policy. Religion, she knows, needs to be taught in the context of history and culture, so combining her class's cultural experiences with an assignment about religion might make an effective WebQuest. But can she design a WebQuest that incorporates higher-level learning and analysis with the specific backgrounds and experiences of her diverse classroom and still maintain the objectivity required? Anita is determined to try! She tries to ignore her hungry, yowling cat as she logs on to QuestGarden at http://www.questgarden.com and signs up for a free trial.

She wants to address technology and social studies standards, so she records the standards in the applicable section of QuestGarden. Her topic will fall under social studies strands I, III, IV, and V. She remembers that NCSS had issued a Position Statement about teaching religion and makes a note to re-review it before creating the assignment. And because the autobiographical essays had highlighted her students' interest in videos and other technology, Anita decides that incorporating filmmaking into the WebQuest task might be interesting to them. In that way, she will be highlighting many of ISTE NETS-S standards. (See Other Resources: D for a mapping of the example WebQuests in this book to the NCSS and ISTE Standards.)

After searching the databases of previously created WebQuests, Anita finds several resources she can use, such as links to information on major world religions, WebQuests about the Israeli/Palestinian conflict, and summaries of features and comparisons of religions—she can save some research time! But none meets her needs completely; she decides to create a unique assignment to address her targeted topic: exploring different religions and the causes of religious conflicts. In researching the impact of religion on the cultures of countries represented by her students, she hopes to find examples that resonate with them personally—and demonstrate that this topic is truly a global issue.

Design Patterns

During the next week, Anita sets aside time to talk to her students individually. She wants to understand the cultural influences on their learning behaviors and what type of assignments would motivate and challenge them. She isn't surprised to discover that, while her students are all proud of their cultures, they are afraid of being singled out in front of their peers. Anita spends extra time with her ESL students to understand their hurdles and what roles and assignments would be comfortable for them. Later, when she logs back on to QuestGarden, she thinks about what she has learned from her conversations.

The set of tools in QuestGarden includes an analysis of standard design patterns that have been proven successful. Each pattern supports different lesson contents and provides the WebQuest with structural cohesiveness. For example, the "Alternative History" design pattern helps students understand cause and effect by having them envision what might have made historical events turn out differently. Selecting a design pattern in QuestGarden assists in organizing the primary components of the WebQuest (Introduction, Task, Process, and Evaluation) according to the content.

Of the twenty-six designs listed, Anita chooses "Policy Briefing"; her student teams will create documentaries, and this pattern focuses on interviewing techniques, evaluating cause and effect, and on creating interpretive presentations. One thing she has learned from her students is that many of them feel ill at ease communicating in groups; scripting and enacting a documentary might encourage them to hone those skills. She also wants to make sure the assignment requires some form of writing, another challenge for many of them.

Take a few minutes to review the twenty-six design patterns, which are organized by type of task at http://webquest.sdsu.edu/designpatterns/all.htm. Examples of types of WebQuests and the purpose of each pattern are contained in a chart. Which patterns best fit the four topics you jotted down earlier and address the needs of your specific learners?

Topic	Design Pattern
1. _____	_____
2. _____	_____
3. _____	_____
4. _____	_____

EXAMPLE WEBQUEST NO. 2: WORLD RELIGIONS AND CONFLICTS

Anita's completed WebQuest is now presented. As we discuss the standard design components in the following chapters, we'll refer back to the applicable component of this assignment. In the next chapter, we'll guide you through developing real and engaging Tasks. Note that the Introduction, which is the component the student sees first, is one of the last pieces developed and will be covered in Chapter 8.

WebQuest

Religious Conflict: Is an End in Sight?

▶ INTRODUCTION

Over the past few months, a number of respected church leaders visited our classroom to discuss the religions they represent and the major religious conflicts that exist today: the continuing Irish debate, the India/Pakistan conflict, and the recent war in the Balkans—and in the past: the Holocaust, the Crusades, and the Spanish Inquisition. Religious conflict can be violent, as with the strife just listed, or it might be a matter of one group excluding or violating the rights of another. Whether the struggles have been on a multi-country scale or isolated within one region, lives on both sides of the conflicts have been significantly impacted. So what *is* religion? What is the underlying cause of conflict "in the name of religion"? And how can future conflicts be avoided? No easy questions! Interestingly, everyone in this class—everyone in the world—has a personal cultural history that has touched on past or current religious conflict.

Now, it is the year 2050 and local and world leaders have come together for a summit on World Peace. I invite all of you to examine some of the histories of conflict in the name of religion—familiar and unfamiliar, current and past—to guide our future world leaders in achieving sustainable peace.

▶ TASK

World leaders have studied the underlying causes of war since the beginning of history and have discovered several consistent themes; one of them is "War in the Name of Religion." They have searched the globe and discovered that our world history class is seeking an understanding of world religions and have asked us to review four religious conflicts to report on the ramifications of those disagreements and to assess similarities and differences regarding the cause of the strife. They have asked us to make a documentary of each of the four conflicts to be studied (**Task 1**) and then present individual papers at the world conference comparing all four (**Task 2**).

▶ PROCESS

Each student will be assigned to one of four groups to study a religious conflict and film a documentary about it. You will need to understand the religions on each side of the strife, as well as the history of the war itself. The four groups are as follows:

I. Islamic/Catholic strife on the island of Mindanao in the Philippines

II. Roman Catholic schism in Brazil (Roman Catholic and Candomblé followers)

III. Arab/Israeli conflict (Islam and Judaism)

IV. Sri Lanka (Hinduism and Buddhism)

Gathering Background Knowledge

Understanding Religion

You will use the notes you've taken from the various guest speakers who have visited us and will access additional information on the Internet. (See the Resources section to find the Internet links for your assigned religion and conflict.) An organizer for summarizing your data is provided now:

	Religion _____	Religion _____
God(s)		
List three primary beliefs		
List three important rituals		
Similarities between the two religions studied (name two to four)		
Differences between the two religions studied (name two to four)		
Founding or important leaders		
Sacred texts		
Sacred symbols		
Place(s) of worship		
Other important observations		

Many of the listed Web sites, especially those discussing the complex issues of religious conflict, are written at an adult comprehension level; for that reason, your role (as either a culture or language specialist) in this assignment will be important to your group. Please read the information in English first, but if you need to translate the site into your native language (and your language is available in the translator facility at http://babelfish.altavista .com/), you may do so after reading the pages in English. You will have two class periods to finish the research portion of this assignment.

Investigating the Assigned Conflict

In your same group, you will read about the conflict assigned to you (see Resources for links to information you will need to review). You should determine the answers to the following questions, which will be used by your group to script and produce the documentary.

- How did the conflict begin?
- What are the key points of disagreement?
- Are they about religion or about something else?
- What factors or incidents exacerbated the conflict?
- How long has the conflict continued?
- Why hasn't the conflict been able to be resolved?

Roles

You will be assigned to a multicultural, multilanguage group. In that group, you will decide what roles should be played in the final documentary and who will play them; but when researching the information for the assignment, half of the group will be language specialists and half will be culture specialists. You will decide among yourselves who will be each, and your choices might surprise you! Work as a team to complete the chart, answer the questions, and film the documentary.

The language experts will

- assist anyone in the group who might have difficulty with English language content and
- prepare the actual script for the documentary.

The culture experts will

- advise the language experts about any particular customs, values, sensitivities, and so on that they need to be aware of while visiting the country to make the documentary and

- make sure the documentary is objective and reflects any cultural considerations that you have advised the language experts on.

Use the following chart to document each team member's role.

	Culture or Language Specialist?	Specific Role in Documentary
Team Member #1:		
Team Member #2:		
Team Member #3:		
Team Member #4:		
Team Member #5:		
Team Member #6:		

Documenting the Problem

Without taking sides, prepare a documentary that educates the public about

- what religion is,
- the religions involved in the conflict, and
- the conflict itself.

Use all members of your team to participate in the documentary, selecting whatever roles you feel are appropriate. Some of these might be interviewer, historian, theologian, economist, translator, or culture expert. Of course, other roles might be more suitable—choose what makes sense and is engaging to your audience! Keep in mind that your documentary will be used by all teams to assess solutions for ending religious conflict. You will have three weeks (mostly outside of class) to script and film the documentary.

Assessing Solutions

Once we have viewed all the documentaries and have had the opportunity to ask the teams questions, you will write an individual essay (two to three double-spaced pages) to present to the world leaders. They have asked us to determine what the underlying causes of religious conflict might be and make recommendations for preventing such strife in the future. Use the following organizer to record your thoughts; you are comparing the four conflicts, not reexamining individual conflicts.

	Conflict I	Conflict II	Conflict III	Conflict IV
Common areas of disagreement				
Unique areas of disagreement				
Economic factors				
Cultural factors: —language —ethics —tradition —other —belief systems				
Geographic factors				
Other factors (list them and assess)				

This essay is due one week after all documentaries have been viewed.

Resources

> *Teacher Note:* In the actual WebQuest, only the name you give to the link (not the URL) would appear to the student.

Religions

Buddhism

- BBC: Religion & Ethics: Buddhism—http://www.bbc.co.uk/religion/religions/buddhism/
- ReligionFacts.com—http://www.religionfacts.com/buddhism/

Candomblé

- BBC: Religion & Ethics: Candomblé—http://www.bbc.co.uk/rcligion/religions/candomble/
- Pilot Destination Guides—http://www.pilotguides.com/destination_guide/south_america/brazil/candomble.php
- Candomblé: Enclyclopedia—http://www.experiencefestival.com/a/Candombl/id/438599

Hinduism

- BBC: Religion & Ethics: Hinduism—http://www.bbc.co.uk/religion/religions/hinduism/
- ReligionFacts.com—http://www.religionfacts.com/hinduism/

Islam

- BBC: Religion & Ethics: Islam—http://www.bbc.co.uk/religion/religions/islam/
- ReligionFacts.com—http://www.religionfacts.com/islam/

Judaism

- BBC: Religion & Ethics: Judaism—http://www.bbc.co.uk/religion/religions/judaism/
- ReligionFacts.com—http://www.religionfacts.com/judaism/

Roman Catholicism

- Beliefnet—http://www.beliefnet.com/story/80/story_8030_1
- ReligionFacts.com—http://www.religionfacts.com/christianity/denominations/catholicism.htm

Conflicts

Islamic/Catholic Strife on the Island of Mindanao in the Philippines

- Center for Reduction of Religious Based Conflict—http://aps.naples.net/community/NFNWebpages/storyboard.cfm?StoryBoardNum=142&PageNum=150
- Peace Forum Paper—http://bugsnbytes.tripod.com/bb_newsletter_0004_02.html
- Asia Source Paper—http://www.asiasource.org/asip/mindanao2004.cfm

Roman Catholic Schism in Brazil

- Center for Reduction of Religious Based Conflict—http://aps.naples.net/community/NFNWebpages/storyboard.cfm?StoryBoardNum=142&PageNum=20
- Worldwide Religious News—http://www.wwrn.org/article.php?idd=16592&sec=39&cont=8
- News Article—http://findarticles.com/p/articles/mi_m1058/is_n35_v114/ai_20114094

Arab/Israeli Conflict

- MSN Encarta—http://encarta.msn.com/encyclopedia_761588322/arab-israeli_conflict.html
- Historyteacher.net—http://www.historyteacher.net/Arab-Israeli_Conflict.htm

Sri Lanka

- Center for Reduction of Religious Based Conflict—http://aps.naples.net/community/NFNWebpages/storyboard.cfm?StoryBoardNum=142&PageNum=160

- Religious Tolerance.org—http://www.religioustolerance.org/rt_srilanka.htm
- BBC article—http://news.bbc.co.uk/2/hi/south_asia/country_profiles/1168427.stm

▶ EVALUATION

TASK 1: Create a Documentary

	Exceeds Standard	Meets Standard	Approaching Standard	Does Not Meet Standard
Research (Individual)	The research came from at least six different sources and was cited correctly.	The research came from three to five different sources and was cited correctly.	The research came from less than three different sources and was cited correctly.	The research was minimal and was not cited or was not cited correctly.
Collaboration (Individual)	The student showed leadership skills and helped keep the group on task.	The student made significant contributions to the group and final product.	The student made some contributions, but allowed other students to assume a greater share of the work.	The student did not make significant contributions to the final product.
Quality of the Documentary (Group)	The documentary was professional. It portrayed the facts without bias and presented a complete view of the topic.	The documentary portrayed the facts without bias and presented a complete view of the topic.	Additional facts are needed to present the complete view of the topic or slight bias is evident.	The topic was not presented completely or was presented in a biased manner.
Use of Technology (Group)	The technology was used in a way that enhanced the overall quality of the documentary.	The technology was appropriate and chosen well.	For the most part, the technology was used well, but in some places lessened the effect of the documentary.	The technology detracted from the overall quality of the documentary.

TASK 2: Present a Paper to World Leaders

	Exceeds Standard	Meets Standard	Approaching Standard	Does Not Meet Standard
Writing Mechanics	There were no errors in grammar, spelling, punctuation, or capitalization.	There were one or two errors in grammar, spelling, punctuation, or capitalization.	There were three or four errors in grammar, spelling, punctuation, or capitalization.	There were five or more errors in grammar, spelling, punctuation, or capitalization.
Support for Argument and Cohesiveness of Argument	The conclusions are well supported by documented facts. The conclusions logically flow from the statements.	The conclusions are supported by documented facts. The conclusions for the most part logically flow from the statements.	Some conclusions are not supported by documented facts. The arguments have some inconsistencies.	The arguments are not well supported. The conclusions lack logic and consistency.
Quantity and Quality of Information	The paper contains many well-cited facts. The sources are reputable.	The paper contains sufficient well-cited facts. The sources are reputable.	Sources were cited, but were not from highly reputable sources. Some opinions were presented as fact.	Sources were not cited. More opinions than facts were presented.

▶ CONCLUSION

Congratulations! You tackled some complicated, and perhaps emotional, issues. As a follow-up to this assignment, after you receive your essay back, think about sharing it with your classmates. We'll set aside some time a few weeks after the assignment has ended to let you read your analysis aloud in class if you so choose.

6 Authentic and Engaging Tasks

Maria Borden is in her fourth year teaching social studies in a large, urban high school in western Texas. Close to thirty percent of the county population was not born in the United States, and over ninety percent of those residents are Hispanic. Maria knows, even from her short experience, that teaching immigration from the textbook doesn't seem to work with her students. It's such a personal and emotional issue for them. Many of her students are not citizens; some might be here illegally. Family members might have been denied job employment opportunities and access to education and training, and in some cases, families had been torn apart.

Maria's class consists of twenty-four students: thirteen are female and eleven are male; fifteen speak primarily Spanish at home and, of these students, three were born in the United States. The remaining nine students speak English at home and have a variety of ethnic backgrounds, including French Canadian, Irish, and Italian.

MEET JUAN PABLO ESCORIZA . . .

My mom said I used to come home from school at three, have something to eat, and then sleep until the next morning when it was time to go to school again. School was exhausting for me. I was nine when my family moved from Mexico to a small town in New York State and I knew no English at all. I sat in school all day without a clue about what everyone was saying. There were no ESL services at the school so my parents signed me up for English lessons. They had me watch movies and TV in English and soon I learned to understand and speak.

The money differences between the United States and Mexico are great. One dollar will give you about ten pesos so money earned in the U.S. can buy a lot. Many times a family member will come to the U.S. just to work so that they can send the money home and give their family a better life. I don't see why people say that immigrants are taking away jobs. They work the jobs that no else wants. My family was fortunate because my father worked for a good company in Mexico. He had to work 24/7 though, so when he was transferred here, he took the opportunity because it meant he could spend more time with the family.

I feel like we study the same stuff over and over again in history classes. I don't know how many times I have learned about World War II. It always seems so biased – "America is great. America is the best." I wish that other students knew more about my history and culture. They celebrate Cinco de Mayo but that is not our Independence Day. It is in September but nobody seems to know that. I think there needs to be more of a world view in History classes so that more students will want to study abroad. There is so much more to learn!

POSING AUTHENTIC PROBLEMS TO CHALLENGE THINKING SKILLS

Maria wants to encourage her students to explore many different issues concerning immigration, from its history and impact on the development of the country to the human rights issues often in the news. It seems to her those very news stories could be the way to engage her students. She also wants students who are not immigrants to understand that the struggles some of their peers are facing are the same issues their own immigrant ancestors might have faced at different times in history. When Juan moved to her school from upper New York state and shared some of his experiences in adjusting to a new country and language, it made her think about her own ancestors who had faced the same struggles many years earlier. Her grandmother, after whom she was named, came from the Azores as a young girl and knew no English. Her mother's grandparents were from Poland and faced the same problems with language and employment that her students' families are facing now.

Maria has decided that this unit is a perfect opportunity to create a WebQuest lesson. In the past, she used WebQuests found on the Internet for other topics and was pleased her students responded well to this type of learning activity. Creating a task to engage her students in higher-level thinking that will pose an authentic problem is Maria's first challenge. She bookmarked a number of online resources on immigration when she taught the topic last year and had found news articles and online videos that depict current problems and opinions on immigration. Based on a colleague's rec-ommendation, she purchased *El Norte,* a film about sibling refugees from Guatemala who travel to Mexico and then to the United States, crossing the border illegally with the help of a coyote (a human smuggler).

BRAINSTORMING WEBQUEST TASKS

As Maria considers options for the WebQuest Task, she decides to incorpo-rate role-playing, a technique that encourages students to view issues from different perspectives. Several tasks came to mind: her students might ben-efit from having a debate or creating a TV news broadcast or other type of show; maybe they could write a newspaper or a blog.

The WebQuest Task, or culminating project, is what separates the WebQuest learning paradigm from a simple Web scavenger hunt. By means of this task, students demonstrate synthesis and application of the informa-tion they absorb. Determining appropriate tasks for a WebQuest is a critical design component. Not only will the task be the activity that will allow the teacher to perform meaningful assessment, but it will also either engage or fail to engage the student in critical thinking and true application of knowl-edge. The challenge teachers face when designing WebQuest Tasks is to make them relevant, meaningful, engaging, and assessable.

In this chapter, we explore tasks that could be integrated into Maria's WebQuest on immigration. When determining a task, start by looking at the lesson's objectives as well as the resources to be used. Also consider student population and available school resources.

We will now examine some of Maria's ideas.

Debates are a good way to engage students, especially if role-playing is a feature of the WebQuest. Students are already exploring the resources from different perspectives and likely forming opinions. Debates might take on the form of a traditional, two-sided debate, a mock political debate between candidates in an election, or even a mock trial in which students argue for opposing sides. Educational factors to be considered are class size, language fluency, and ensuring all students have meaningful ways to participate. Considering the demographics of Maria's class, what do you consider the strong points in favor of using a debate?

_____

_____

_____

Do you see any potential problems with this task?

_____

_____

_____

We mentioned several types of debates above. Which type would you be most likely to consider? Why?

_____

_____

_____

Another possibility is creating a newscast or other type of show. Maria's school recently purchased several digital video recorders, and she has been interested in finding creative ways to integrate video production into the curriculum. One way to define the task would be to have students create an evening newscast about a recent factory raid. Because role-playing is an effective WebQuest strategy, one student in each group could be the newscaster, another could be the "on the scene" reporter, a third could be a government official, a fourth could be a worker who has been arrested, a fifth could be the factory owner, and a sixth person could be from a local church group that has been advocating for local immigrants. Since Maria has twenty-four students in her class, four groups would research and plan newscasts. And if each group planned and videotaped a five-minute newscast, students would be able to view and critique all of them within a single class period.

What suggestions would you give Maria? Would you consider different or additional roles?

_____

_____

_____

What other types of TV programs might students create?

_____

_____

_____

When using digital video in the classroom, consider all technical aspects, such as availability of hardware and software, learning time if students are not familiar with the process, and the cost of supplies and media.

If another classroom goal is providing more opportunities for students to write, a teacher might consider tasks that relate to print journalism, such as newspapers, magazines, or even blogs. Because many of Maria's students receive ESL services, she tries to encourage process writing and peer review in her assignments whenever possible.

If you were to consider using a newspaper format, what types of tasks would you design?

_____

_____

_____

_____

What would be the software and supply requirements for the tasks you designed?

_____

_____

_____

_____

If you wanted to have students create magazine components instead, what additional considerations would you have?

_____

_____

_____

_____

Web logs, or *blogs,* have rapidly gained in popularity. A blog can be used to provide news or comments, and because it is Web-based, it has the advantage of allowing links, audio, and video in addition to text and images. As with any public presence on the Internet, a teacher needs to consider privacy and safety issues. Included at the end of this chapter are resources on Internet safety, as well as information on blogs specifically designed for educational use.

What suggestions would you give Maria if she chose to have students create a blog? How might students be grouped or assigned roles?

_____

_____

_____

What other tasks do you think might be engaging and relevant for Maria's class?

_____

_____

_____

Exercises: Tasks From Example WebQuests in Previous Chapters

Frank Parker's students (Chapter 3) documented data in an organizer and presented their findings by creating a PowerPoint presentation. How else might they communicate their analysis? What approach might generate more discussion or debate among the teams?

_____

_____

_____

Another way to study recent African history and political climate is through fiction. What tasks would you create for students who have just read books such as *The Heinemann Book of Contemporary African Short Stories* or Peter Dickinson's *AK?* (See Other Resources: C at the end of this book for help in finding good, young adult reading.)

_____

_____

_____

Anita Bertz considered teaching religion in the context of music, art, or architecture in Chapter 5. The Minnesota State University's online "Religions of the World Museum" is located at http://www.mnsu.edu/emuseum/cultural. What tasks could be developed for such a WebQuest?

_____

_____

_____

Another way to study religion is to read religious texts, many of which can be accessed at Religion Online at http://www.religion-online.org/. What tasks could you develop for your classroom using this approach?

_____

_____

_____

What other approaches and tasks could be used to study religion in a culturally responsive way?

_____

_____

_____

Chart of Possible Tasks

Here are some suggestions for the types of tasks you might develop, but don't be limited by these—the possibilities are numerous!

Task Category	Suggestions
Multimedia	Filmed documentaries, newscasts, TV shows, multimedia presentations such as PowerPoint or Web pages
Written	Newspapers, blogs, persuasive essays, film scripts, plays, journals, poems, short stories
Oral Presentations	Debates, political speeches, plays, minilessons
Other	Models, simulations, photographs

Online Resources

The following sites might be helpful to you in developing WebQuest Tasks:

SDSU College of Education

● The SDS Taskonomy Web page describes twelve different categories of tasks and provides suggestions as well as links to WebQuests—http://webquest.sdsu.edu/taskonomy.html

Internet Safety

A number of sites provide links and information about Internet safety:

● http://www.netsmartz.org/
● http://www.isafe.org/
● http://www.safekids.com/
● http://www.fbi.gov/publications/pguide/pguidee.htm
● http://www.safeteens.com/

Blogs

● The University of Houston at Clear Lake blogs page provides links to articles, sample blogs, and blog-writing tools—http://awd.cl.uh.edu/blog/
● The information page at *wiredsafety.com* provides general information on blog safety as well as specific details about sites such as MySpace and YouTube—http://www.wiredsafety.org/internet101/blogs.html
● The blog resources at *Epals.com* allow teachers and students to participate in safe and protected collaboration—http://schoolblog.epals.com/
● The article on Emerging Technologies in the online journal *Language Learning and Technology* provides information about blogs and wikis—http://llt.msu.edu/vol7num2/emerging/default.html

EXAMPLE WEBQUEST NO. 3:
IMMIGRATION: PAST, PRESENT, AND FUTURE

Maria's WebQuest follows. As we continue to discuss the standard design components in the next several chapters, we'll refer back to the applicable components of this assignment. Chapter 7 guides you through developing rubrics that will facilitate objective Evaluations for WebQuest Tasks.

WebQuest

Lights, Camera, Action!
An Immigration Perspective

▶ INTRODUCTION

The film *El Norte* tells the story of Rosa and Enrique, siblings who are Mayan Indians from Guatemala. After their father is killed by government soldiers, they realize he was right when he said their government just considered them "arms" to serve the needs of those in power, so they decide to seek a better life in the North (El Norte). This film is set in 1983, and while a few things have changed, much has not. You and your production team will have the opportunity to propose a sequel to *El Norte*, set in the present day.

▶ TASK

You will be working in groups of six to research and plan a proposed sequel to *El Norte*. After we view the film as a class, your group will investigate certain aspects of immigration history in the United States, immigration laws, and related humanitarian concerns. In each group, two students will be historians, two will be lawyers, and two will be social service workers. After each group performs the necessary research, you will draft your movie proposal as a team. Each team will pitch its proposal to an elite group of movie executives, who look remarkably like the social studies teachers in our school! A contract will be awarded to the best proposal.

▶ PROCESS

After we view *El Norte*, you will have two class periods to complete your research in the computer lab. Here is a list of suggested resources, including specific links for each role. You may use additional credible Web resources if you wish.

> *Teacher Note:* Immigration information changes continuously, and the Internet facilitates access to the most current information because it is a fluid resource. Many of the topics you teach are likely subject to similar change, and WebQuests are an effective way to address those topics and themes with fresh and relevant information.

General Immigration Resources

The Immigration Debate
- http://www.npr.org/templates/story/story.php?storyId=5310549
- http://www.immigration-usa.com/debate.html

Labor history in the United States (resource links)
- http://www.kentlaw.edu/ilhs/curricul.htm

Wikipedia Resources
- http://en.wikipedia.org/wiki/Immigration_to_the_United_States

An Interview with the Director of *El Norte*
- http://www.lib.berkeley.edu/MRC/NavaInterview.html

Mexican Immigration
- http://memory.loc.gov/learn/features/immig/mexican.html

Web Resources for Historians

U.S. Immigration History from Rapidimmigration.com
- http://www.rapidimmigration.com/usa/1_eng_immigration_history.html

University of Minnesota Immigration History Research Center
- http://www.ihrc.umn.edu/

Historical Views of Immigration
- http://www.cis.org/articles/cantigny/fonte.html

A History of U.S. Immigration (America's Heritage Exhibit)
● http://www.ailf.org/exhibit/ex_americasheritage_traveling/
  traveling_exhibit.shtml

Web Resources for Lawyers

Migration Information Resources
● http://www.migrationinformation.org/

U.S. Immigration Laws
● http://www.uscis.gov/portal/site/uscis

A History of U.S. Immigration (America's Heritage Exhibit)
● http://www.ailf.org/exhibit/ex_americasheritage_traveling/
  traveling_exhibit.shtml

Web Resources for Social Service Workers

Immigrant Voices from University of Houston Digital History Site
● http://www.digitalhistory.uh.edu/historyonline/ethnic_am.cfm

Humanitarian Parole
● http://immigration.about.com/od/asylumrefugees/g/humpar.htm

Interviews With Immigrants
● http://memory.loc.gov/learn/features/immig/interv/toc.php

Once your research is complete, your group will have one class period to outline your proposal and another period to draft it. Here are some guidelines that will help you prepare your document:

1. Give the proposed sequel a title and describe the setting (place and year).
2. List the main characters and describe each in a sentence or two. You must include characters whose viewpoints or experiences represent the information you have found in your research.
3. Summarize the plot in one paragraph.
4. Elaborate on the plot with a three-page narrative. The narrative must include supporting information from all three areas of your research. For example, you might decide that Enrique has been allowed to remain in the United States legally and have flashbacks to the court case that decided his fate. Or you might describe a sequel in which Enrique returns to Mexico or Guatemala. What did the historians, the lawyers, and the social services professionals find out that need to be portrayed in the new storyline?

▶ EVALUATION

Your proposal will be evaluated on the following criteria:

1. Does it contain all the required elements (1 to 4 above) in sufficient detail?
2. Is your supporting documentation adequate and does your proposal reflect the information you found?
3. Is your proposal well organized?
4. Is it creative and interesting?
5. Does your oral presentation engage your audience?
6. Were you able to answer all questions posed by the "movie executives"?

The following rubrics will help you prepare your written and oral presentations and will be used by the reviewers to provide feedback for your group.

Proposal Rubric

	4	3	2	1
Proposal Elements	The required elements (title, setting, and character descriptions) are included and detailed.	The required elements (title, setting, and character descriptions) are included. More details would be an improvement.	One required element is missing or the details are insufficient.	Descriptions are not clear or are missing.
Summary	The paragraph is well written, without errors. The plot is evident.	The paragraph is basically well written, but contains one or two errors. The plot is evident.	The paragraph contains three or more errors. The plot is somewhat confusing.	The paragraph contains four or more errors. The plot is not clear.
Creativity	The proposal is original and very creative.	The proposal is original.	The proposal lacks originality.	The proposal shows little thought.
Accuracy and Research	The proposal uses the research very effectively and events to be included in the sequel relate well to the research.	The proposal uses the research to determine the events that will be included in the sequel.	The proposal uses the research somewhat. More facts need to be included.	The use of the research is not evident in the proposal.

Oral Presentation Rubric

	4	3	2	1
Presentation Effectiveness and Professionalism	The group was very professional and presented their proposal clearly.	The proposal was presented in a reasonably clear and professional manner.	More details are needed in the presentation, and some details were not clear.	The group's demeanor was not professional. Lack of details made it difficult to determine what the proposal was about.
Responses to Questions	Responses demonstrated that the group was very familiar with the facts and had given serious thought to the events in the proposed sequel. Answers were detailed.	Responses were good, contained adequate detail, and related to the research.	The group seemed confused at times. Responses were incomplete.	Responses indicated that group was not familiar with the facts found during the research phase.
Use of Visuals or Technology	The visuals and technology made a strong positive impact.	The visuals and technology were effective.	Some visuals and technology were used, but did not have a strong effect.	No visuals or technology were used.

▶ CONCLUSION

Congratulations! Your career in historical fiction and filmmaking is off to a great start! The history and impact of immigration in the United States is multifaceted, as you have learned from your own research and from hearing what the other groups accomplished. Immigrants face common issues, whether they enter the country legally or illegally, and even when they are invited to the United States as part of a refugee program. Are you curious about the refugee experience in America? A more recent film, the documentary *Lost Boys of Sudan,* follows two orphaned boys who were brought to the United States by INS from war-torn East Africa. After watching this film, write a few notes in a journal about what made the American experience better, the same, and worse for these refugees versus Rosa and Enrique's immigration.

7 Evaluation Rubrics

Evaluation of student work, especially when it represents creative tasks, can be challenging. Standards answer the question "What do my students need to know and be able to do?" while the Evaluation tells us whether they have mastered the lesson. In this chapter, we examine methods of appraising the results of the WebQuest Task by using well-designed rubrics that will

- allow students to perform formative self-assessment as they complete the task and
- facilitate your process of performing equitable summative assessment of the assignment.

Ron Kowal has taught social studies in a Chicago suburb for over twenty years. He has become increasingly aware of the need to prepare his students to live in a global community and be able to use new technology tools. The presence of universities and industry in the area has resulted in the student population at his school becoming more representative of the world at large. A number of his students are first-generation immigrants from countries in Eastern Europe.

MEET VLADIMIR EMILOV EVTIMOV . . .

When I was six and half years old my family moved from Bulgaria to Russia and I started first grade there. The teachers there basically ignored my Bulgarian heritage but even though, they really stimulated me to learn, especially to learn a foreign language. Foreign languages were required and I chose English. I liked going to school there. I think that the collapse of the Soviet Union allowed the schools to offer a more creative curriculum and much broader and challenging one too. I remember studying mythology, logic and I really liked math.

But, my experience here in the United States was good as well. One of my best memories was Ms. H's American history class last year. She took time with me and helped me to be involved in the class. When we were studying World War I and II, she expected a lot from me. She always asked me to tell the class about my experience in Bulgaria, what I knew about Bulgaria's involvement in the wars and what I thought. She always asked me to help students with the geography of Bulgaria and Europe and they would help me with the geography of the U.S. I was really happy to have this opportunity to share my voice.

Ron teaches world geography to sophomores. National Geography Standard One from the National Geographic Society addresses spatial perspective with an emphasis on the use of maps and other geographic representations, tools, and technologies. Ron previously used WebQuests in his U.S. history classes, and he decides this would be a good method for students to gain experience using emerging technologies for geography lessons. He knows the Internet has helped Vladi remain connected to Bulgaria, and Vladi's classmates have expressed interest in learning more about Eastern Europe. Because he always begins his geography curriculum with lessons on creating and using maps, Ron decides to integrate his students' personal backgrounds and interests with this activity to make it more compelling for them.

Ron had suffered through high school geography—it was so boring! He had to memorize not only the shapes of the countries to identify them on maps, but also capitals and resources. He never imagined being able to travel to any of those places, so the tasks seemed meaningless. Encouraging students to explore maps and other resources on the Internet, and then create their own country and map using what they have learned just might spark their interest. Learning more about the world regions they needed to study would be a less transparent aspect of the lesson. Activities ranging from zooming in on satellite images using Google Earth to exploring interactive railway maps would create a varied and rich set of experiences for his students. Things had certainly come a long way from when he was in school, with printed maps and globes being the only resources available.

USING RUBRICS

Understandably, Ron finds objective assessment of shared or creative tasks a bit challenging. From past assignments, he has also seen that students produce far better work when they unmistakably comprehend what is expected. Using rubrics, the standard tool of WebQuest Evaluations, can accomplish both objectivity and clarity. Students can refer to the rubric as they create an assignment, employing formative self-assessment by checking whether their work is in line with expectations at each stage of the project. It can also help them perform peer reviews on others' work. From the teacher's perspective, a well-designed rubric contains measurable descriptors that make student assessment easier and more objective. For group work, which is more difficult to judge on an individual basis, peer reviews can be incorporated into the rubric, or if the group work is done during class, you can interact with and observe each group's work to help form your assessment.

Online Tools

Online tools and resources have taken much of the work out of creating effective rubrics. Some sites that contain sample rubrics are included near the end of this chapter, before the example WebQuest. Two free sites allowing teachers to create and save rubrics are Rubistar (http://rubistar.4teachers .org/index.php) and Teach-nology (http://www.teach-nology.com/web_tools/ rubrics/). Take some time now to explore these sites, and write your comments on the following lines. What are the best features of each? What limitations do you find?

_____

_____

_____

_____

How Many Rubrics?

In Ron's geography WebQuest, students will be cartographers, creating a map of a newly formed Eastern European country designed specifically for a target audience. Once students have completed initial research as a group, Ron will assign design specifications and individual roles to the students. Three research roles will focus on three different types of data the group decides are important for their map, and one student will assume the role of statistician. This role will be responsible for calculating the map scale, determining the longitude and latitude of the new country, and planning the general map size. One thing Ron considers is how many rubrics to create. Should there be separate evaluations for each role? Should the creation of the map be assessed separately from the classroom presentation? Record your thoughts.

_____

_____

_____

Rubric Dimensions and Scale

Ron determines that he will create one rubric to assess the map and presentation, and then create separate rubrics for each team member according to role. After deciding to apply the four-point scale commonly used at his school, his next task is to determine the dimensions he will evaluate. What are some of the points you would assess on the map and the presentation?

_____

_____

_____

Once the dimensions are determined, descriptors for each scale value must be written. Ron's final rubrics are included in the example WebQuest at the end of this chapter, but for now let's look at one of the dimensions for the map. Ron wants to make certain the information included on the map meets the needs of the target audience. This is what he has designed.

	_4_	_3_	_2_	_1_
Map Content	The map includes at least three different kinds of information that will be helpful to the audience.	The map includes two different kinds of information that will be helpful to the audience.	The map includes only one kind of information that will be helpful to the audience.	The information on the map does not relate to the needs of the audience.

Notice that the wording is general enough to apply to each map, but also measurable so that students and teacher will be able to determine the quality of the content. Another aspect Ron wants to assess is the scale used in the map. First, consider what is necessary for the map scale to be useful and correct and jot down your ideas.

_____

_____

_____

Next, add descriptors to the grid to show how you would assess the dimension of Map Scale.

	4	3	2	1
Map Scale				

Because Ron wants to create a separate rubric for each role, he needs to determine his expectations. The statistician must calculate an appropriate scale for the map as well as gather the longitude and latitude data needed for inclusion. What would you consider important dimensions for the statistician's rubric?

_____

_____

_____

Exercises: Evaluation Rubrics From Example WebQuests

Let's look at a portion of the rubrics created to assess WebQuest Tasks in previous chapters.

In Frank Parker's Zambia WebQuest, the quality of data, maps, charts, and images was weighted 10 percent of the total assessment.

	4	3	2	1
Data 10%	The data presented supports the topic well. The graph represents the data in a clear and meaningful way.	The data presented supports the topic well. The graph represents the data but is not clear.	The data supports the topic, but is not complete. More data is needed.	The data does not support the topic.

How would you revise this portion of the evaluation to make it more measurable?

_____

_____

_____

Anita Bertz used two different rubrics for the WebQuest she created on world religions in Chapter 5—one for the documentary and another for the written paper. The rubric for the documentary included some items to be assessed for the individual students and other items for the group work. How would you have designed rubrics for her WebQuest? Note options.

_____

_____

_____

This is the scale for the quality and quantity of information in the written paper. Why might this dimension be difficult to judge? What words make the descriptions vague?

	4	3	2	1
Quantity and Quality of Information	The paper contains many well-cited facts. The sources are reputable.	The paper contains sufficient well-cited facts. The sources are reputable.	Sources were cited, but were not from highly reputable sources. Some opinions were presented as fact.	Sources were not cited. More opinions than facts were presented.

Try revising this section of the rubric to make it more measurable.

	4	3	2	1
Quantity and Quality of Information				

Are there any other changes or additions you would make to Anita's rubrics? List them.

_____

_____

_____

Maria Borden also chose to use two rubrics for her WebQuest on Immigration in Chapter 6. One assessed the written proposal and the other evaluated the group oral presentation. Students were assigned WebQuest roles, but the assessment is for only the group results. What problems might this cause? How would you create individual evaluations?

_____

_____

_____

Maria could have required the students to use a specific technology application for the oral report—perhaps a PowerPoint presentation. What dimensions would you assess in that case? How would you make the descriptions measurable?

_____

_____

_____

Note that Anita used scales to describe the performance related to standards (Exceeds Standards, Meets Standards, etc.) while Frank, Maria, and Ron used a numeric scale. Do you see any benefits of using one over the other? Sometimes rubrics will list the lowest performance on the left (e.g., 1 to 4 instead of 4 to 1). What are your thoughts about the order of the scale?

_____

_____

_____

As you create rubrics to assess the tasks your students perform in a WebQuest, keep in mind to

- limit the number of dimensions to a manageable number (four to six) and size of the rubric to a single Web page if possible;
- create separate rubrics for different tasks (written work, oral presentations);
- make the descriptors measurable by using specific numbers rather than general terms like *few* or *many*;
- write the rubrics in language your students will understand so that they can use it as they complete the task;
- determine what worked well and what was unclear, missing, or unnecessary; and
- revise your rubrics before you use them in subsequent assignments.

Online Resources

The following resources will be helpful in creating WebQuest Evaluations; also included are links to free printable maps and geography standards:

SDSU College of Education

- WebQuest Assessment—http://webquest.sdsu.edu/rubrics/weblessons.htm

Sample Rubrics and Resources

- Rubrics4Teachers—http://www.rubrics4teachers.com/
- Kathy Schrock's Guide on Discovery.com—http://school.discovery.com/schrockguide/assess.html

---

Online Sources of Free Printable Maps

- http://www.nationalgeographic.com/xpeditions/atlas/
- http://geography.about.com/library/blank/blxeurope.htm
- http://www.enchantedlearning.com/geography/europe/outlinemap/
- http://www.printablemaps.net/europe-maps/
- http://maps.hist-geo.com/Europe/Outline/

National Geographic

- National Geography Standards—http://www.nationalgeographic.com/resources/ngo/education/standardslist.html

---

EXAMPLE WEBQUEST NO. 4: EFFECTIVE USE OF GEOGRAPHIC TOOLS

After reviewing Ron Kowal's example geography assignment, we'll move on to explore the details of the WebQuest Process in the next chapter.

WebQuest

Calling All Cartographers!

▶ **INTRODUCTION**

You and your design team have been commissioned to prepare a map of the newly formed country of Gizmonia in Eastern Europe. This map will be used by a group of entrepreneurs who hired you to determine how to build and market their company in the new nation. Because Gizmonia was created as a utopian society using land generously donated by existing Eastern European nations, you will need to make sure that your map accurately portrays the conditions of the area, including longitude and latitude, land forms, resources, and population. Your final map will be included in the new *Atlas of Eastern European Countries.*

▶ TASK

Your team will investigate different types of maps and geographic represen-tations used to convey information about the geography of a region. You will use some of the new interactive tools available on the Internet. During this exploration, you need to take notes on what kind of information is available, how it is represented, and which methods seem to you to be the clearest and most effective.

After your team completes the research and exploration phase, you will create a map of the newly formed country of Gizmonia. Your drawing must include at least three types of information important to your client. Each team will have a different client group assigned by the world leader (aka Mr. Kowal). Each person will have a unique role within the team in the research and creation of your particular map. Be as creative as you like, but make sure you use the guidelines provided so that your map is both useful and complete. Once all the maps have been created, they will be presented to the rest of the class, who will then take on the role of the company that hired you.

▶ PROCESS

Background for All Teams

As we explore the use of maps and geographic representations, we will use some of the countries in the area of the world known as Eastern Europe for our research. If you are not familiar with Eastern Europe, your group should *first look at* the interactive puzzle map found at http://www .yourchildlearns.com/map-puzzles.htm. Click on Europe and play the version that has countries with outlines. For further information, you can explore the Europe quiz at http://www.lizardpoint.com/fun/geoquiz/euroquiz.html and the information at http://en.wikipedia.org/wiki/Geography_of_Europe. Your group should not spend more than fifteen minutes exploring these sites (no matter how much fun the puzzle is!). By the end of this initial review, you should have the names of the countries filled in on your map.

> *Teacher Note:* A blank outline map of Eastern Europe will be pro-vided to each student. Sources for free, printable maps are included in the Online Resources textbox earlier in this chapter.

The *second phase* of your research involves learning more about Eastern European countries using online maps and tools. Click on the following links to gather as much information as you can about the different countries. Record your findings on the graphic organizer provided.

> *Teacher Note:* A graphic organizer or chart will help the students keep track of the different types of maps and tools, where they found them, and the features of each. This can be especially helpful for struggling readers, students whose first language is not English, or students who have difficulty taking notes. You can create organizers using a tool such as Inspiration® or a word processor. If you are not familiar with graphic organizers, or if you have not used them in your classroom, you can find samples of organizers at http://www.eduplace.com/graphicorganizer/ and http://inspiration.com/.

Research Links

Eastern Europe Maps and Resources

- REC—Regional Environment Center—http://www.rec.org/REC/Maps/eur_map.html
- United Nations Environment Program Maps and Graphics—http://maps.grida.no/
- Google Earth (Note: This has been downloaded to your computer. Use the icon on your desktop.)
- Alexandria Digital Library—http://www.alexandria.ucsb.edu/other-sites/Europe.html
- Map Collection of Perry Castañeda—http://www.lib.utexas.edu/maps/atlas_east_europe/atlas_e._europe.html
- Statistics—http://www.lib.msu.edu/ticklet/staff/statistics.htm
- Interactive railway map of Europe—http://downloads.raileurope.com/map_europe/europe.html
- National Geographic Map Machine—http://plasma.nationalgeographic.com/mapmachine/
- National Geographic Student Atlas—http://java.nationalgeographic.com/studentatlas/
- Map Scale Calculator—http://www.beg.utexas.edu/GIS/tools/scale2.htm

Phase three of your project will be to create a map for a group of entrepreneurs that has hired your consulting group. Each team will receive a request, provided by your teacher, from one of the following:

○ A large, international *Manufacturing Company* wants to set up a new factory in Gizmonia. You will need to design a map that will help the company plan where to locate their new plant.
○ The newly formed *Gizmonia Department of Tourism* needs a map to help market the interesting features of the country to tourists.
○ A *Major Airline* wants to build an airport in Gizmonia. They need to know where to build to make it successful.
○ The *Gizmonia Agricultural Society* wants to provide advice for farmers on what kinds of crops will grow well and where to plant them, as well as other information necessary for successful farming.
○ A major *University* in the United States wants to build a satellite campus in Gizmonia. They are trying to decide where to build it, as well as what kinds of programs will interest area residents.

Your steps in the design process are as follows:

1. Each student should read the map-making guidelines from National Geographic found at http://www.nationalgeographic.com/ xpeditions/lessons/09/g912/cartographyguidestudent.pdf. You will use the information in this document to make certain your map contains all required components.
2. Request an audience with the world leader to receive your client's specifications and general role assignment (as researcher or statistician) for each team member. Using the map that you labeled in the initial research, draw a rectangle that will become the new country of Gizmonia. It must include land from at least three different actual Eastern European countries. As a team, brainstorm what information will be important to the organization that hired you. You will need to research the areas of the countries that make

up Gizmonia so that your map will be accurate. Use the grading rubrics provided to be sure you are gathering enough information and presenting it correctly. Good collaboration among the group will result in the best product.

3. The world leader assigned three of the students in your group to be researchers and one to be a statistician. The roles and responsibilities are as follows:

   o The *Researchers* will use the organizers already completed and gather additional, specific information on the types of data to be included on your map. Each researcher will concentrate on one of the three types of information your group decides is important.

   o The *Statistician* will determine the scale (use the scale calculator link) that will be used and the longitude and latitude of the country; plan the size, symbols, and colors of the map; and compile any other statistics that are needed. You will also need to verify that thc scale is accurate on the final copy.

Once each team member has completed the individual research, draw the map of Gizmonia together. The *final phase* of your project will be to present the map you created to the organization that hired you (represented by the other members of our class). You should be prepared to answer any questions posed by the group and explain why you chose to include the information you did.

▶ EVALUATION

Your project will be evaluated based upon the final map and the oral presentation. In addition, group members will be assessed on the role they played. The following rubrics will help you as you complete the project. The first rubric will be used to assess your group as a whole, while the other rubrics will be used to assess each individual. Your final grade will be based on the total points you receive from both rubrics.

Map and Oral Presentation Rubric—Group Rubric

	4	3	2	1
Map Content (10 points)	The map includes at least three different kinds of information that will be helpful to the audience.	The map includes two different kinds of information that will be helpful to the audience.	The map includes only one kind of information that will be helpful to the audience.	The information on the map does not relate to the needs of the audience.
Components (10 points)	All **DOGTAIL** components are included.	One or two components are missing, but do not impact the overall usefulness.	Missing components result in the map being less useful.	Important components are missing.
Accuracy (10 points)	All information is correct.	There are one or two minor errors, but they do not impact the overall accuracy of the map.	There are three or more errors or the errors impact the usefulness of the map.	Errors make the map not useful to the audience.
Organization (5 points)	The presenters were very well prepared.	The presenters were sufficiently prepared.	The presenters did not present the details in an organized and logical manner.	The presenters did not seem prepared.
Responses (10 points)	All questions were answered correctly and supported by data.	All questions were answered correctly but not all were supported by data.	Some questions were answered incorrectly or not supported by data.	Responses were not satisfactory.
Demeanor (5 points)	The presenters spoke clearly and in a professional manner.	The presenters were difficult to hear.	The ideas were not presented in a clear manner.	The presentation was not professional.

Researcher Rubric

	4	3	2	1
Accuracy (25 points)	All data was accurate.	There were one or two minor errors that did not impact the overall useful-ness of the map.	There were more than minor errors.	Errors impacted the usefulness of the map.
Sources (25 points)	All sources were credible and cited.	All sources were cited, but some were not credible.	Some or all citations missing or some sources were not credible.	Sources were not credible and were not cited.

Statistician Rubric

	4	3	2	1
Artistic Elements (20 points)	The color, symbols, and other elements make the intent clear.	Choice of color or use of symbols detracts from the overall effect.	The meaning of the map was less clear due to artistic elements.	The map was not neatly drawn and was unclear.
Scale Used (15 points)	The scale was appropriate and calculated correctly.	There was an error in choos-ing the scale or in the cal-culation.	The scale was not appropriate or correct.	No scale was used.
Longitude and Latitude (15 points)	Longitude and latitude were correct for the area chosen.	There were minor errors in representation of longitude and latitude.	Longitude and latitude errors were more serious.	Longitude and latitude were not included.

▶ CONCLUSION

Congratulations! Your consulting team has been awarded the contract to produce the official map for the organization that hired you. It will now be included in the Gizmonia section of the *Atlas of Eastern European Countries*. Your success in creating and understanding the use of maps and other geographic tools will be important to carry forward in new assignments during the remainder of the semester.

8 The WebQuest Process

How, What, and When

You know what lesson you want to teach, have a sense of the final project, and have determined how you'll evaluate the students' work. Now, the WebQuest Process can be fully developed. The Process tells students

- **how** they will work (what teams will be formed, what roles they might play, and what portions of the work will be done individually);
- **what** information they need to assimilate (e.g., a narrative of background information, questions to be answered, links to Internet resources, and access to other study material such as films, books, etc.); and
- **when** the project will be performed and completed.

One of the reasons Jared Zawod loves using WebQuests in his classroom is its emphasis on real-world problem solving. He hates being a Talking Head, spewing out data like the computer on Star Trek! The emphasis on organizing information ahead of time lets him concentrate on his students while they're learning and solving problems; he can focus on helping them grow to become good citizens. That's why he wanted to become a teacher— to make a difference in these kids' lives. He enjoys his ninth-grade civics class, especially instilling in his students enough of an appreciation for their future right to vote that they'll take the responsibility seriously when the time comes. However, he didn't realize how rote his lesson plan had become until this semester.

MEET HASEENA NIAZI . . .

"Don't worry my dear, it will happen in Afghanistan." Those were my brother Ebrahim's words when I told him about the opportunities I have in the United States. I miss my brother. He is an engineer back in my country and he has respect for women. When I first came here ten months ago, everything was so different for me. The clothes, the culture, and the way students acted in the classroom—everything was very different. I was excited about the possibilities, but I was afraid at times too! The first time I saw people drunk, I was frightened. They were yelling and I was thinking they might hurt me. People don't drink like that in Afghanistan. The class-room seemed very strange also. We respect our teachers very much. In class we sit quietly and raise our hands before we say anything. Even if someone is one year older, we have respect for them. When I heard a student call the teacher by his first name, I was waiting for the teacher to throw him out of the room! I thought, "Do I want to stay in a classroom like this where students do not respect the teacher?"

When I was in Afghanistan, I never dreamed that I would get to come to the United States to study. I am so excited about these opportunities that I am getting very interested in human rights. In Afghanistan, when we were under the Taliban, we were told everything, even what we had to wear. When you tell a woman what to wear, you take away her rights! I don't talk much in class about these things, but I do write about them in my papers.

The teachers have been very helpful. Some of them know about Afghanistan and others have tried to find out more about my country. They make a special effort to support me, but I don't want to be treated differently. Some of the students are curious about my country. They asked me—how do you get home? Does Afghanistan have an airport? That seemed so funny to me. I decided to give a presentation about my country and tell about its history and culture and resources. The other students really liked that. I think having international students is like having a living book about their country!

When Haseena asked Jared if she could talk about her country in class, he was surprised. She had spoken little during the first few weeks of the term. Jared realized he had assumed she was shy or her language skills were weak, and now he was a bit angry with himself that he hadn't taken the time to understand Haseena and her culture. Neither of his notions about her had been even close to accurate. After the class presentation, Jared followed up with Haseena about her interest in human rights and learned more about Afghan women's fears even in the current democracy. He had planned to teach about voting rights in a few weeks, and Haseena eagerly agreed that including her country's struggle in his lesson plan would be acceptable to her. It would also help introduce the larger human rights issues of Afghanistan in a way that felt safe to Haseena.

Jared had thought about using a WebQuest to teach voting rights, and now he was even more excited about the opportunity that type of lesson would present. He spent the next few evenings researching and then drafted the Task and the Evaluation Rubric. Now, he's ready to work on the details of the Process.

TEAMS AND ROLES

Team collaboration is an important skill to develop in preparation for the work environment, and Jared knows it also motivates most of his students to do their best. But a team structure can create problems as well, particularly if the workload is unfairly distributed (either by the students themselves or—perish the thought!—by the instructor). For that reason, Jared carefully considers the amount and level of work assigned to each role to challenge every student and meet his or her individual learning goals. Once he knows what roles he wants to assign, he can determine the number of teams that will work on the WebQuest. He ponders the following factors in creating the assignments:

- **Roles** should be important and well defined. What each student will do, and when, must be clear, and each role needs to be an equal and critical contributor to the task. Each role often has distinct resources to review from its own perspective. And when the various roles represent competing points of view, achievement of higher-level thinking is encouraged.
- **Teams** should be equal in size and can work on the same assignment or different aspects of the assignment; for example, all teams might be writing a constitution for a new country, or each team might be designing a constitution for a specific country based on different guidelines. Because all teamwork must be presented and assessed, the number of teams should be manageable (i.e., many teams with only two or three roles might not be the optimal configuration). How the team members will work together in the specified activities must be clear. And there must be specific guidance on how to perform the task(s) to be evaluated.

One of the issues in setting up roles with competing viewpoints is that some might be viewed as "good" and some as "bad." How would you communicate competing roles so that the benefits, but not the drawbacks, are emphasized?

_____

_____

_____

Think about the ways you would evaluate the teamwork component of the assignment. How could you determine whether all members contributed fairly to the team project?

_____

_____

_____

How could you use roles and teams in your classroom to demonstrate the benefits of diversity (i.e., different approaches and methods of contribution) in a work group?

_____

_____

_____

Exercises: Teams and Roles from Example WebQuests

Review the roles and resources from Example WebQuest No. 1 (One Zambia, One Nation?) in Chapter 3. Note that the same resources are assigned to every role. What are the pros and cons of this approach?

Pros	Cons

What methods did Frank Parker use to set clear expectations for each role? Is any aspect of "how, what, and when" unclear?

_____

_____

_____

Anita Bertz chose a different approach to assigning roles in Chapter 5 for the Religious Conflicts WebQuest. She had specialized roles (for language and culture) and asked students to create and assign roles for producing the documentary. What do you see as the pros and cons of these approaches?

	Pros	**Cons**

Specialized Roles _____

_____

_____

_____

Students Determine Roles _____

_____

_____

_____

Anita wasn't surprised to learn that her students, while proud of their heritages, didn't want to feel "singled out." How do you think she should manage the discussion of the "specialized roles" so that her students don't feel embarrassed?

_____

_____

_____

Review the resources assigned to each role in Chapter 6 (the immigration assignment). Did Maria Borden provide enough information for each role to allow the students to analyze immigration issues from the distinct perspectives? Are resources fairly allocated among roles? What would you change, if anything?

_____

_____

_____

Maria also assigned duplicate roles within the same team. What do you see as the pros and cons of this approach?

_____

_____

_____

CHOOSING APPROPRIATE RESOURCES

Although Jared explored many Internet sites while determining his lesson topic and formulating the Task and Assessment, he needs to evaluate and finalize every bit of information his students will access during the Process component. Creating this phase of the lesson takes the most time, so he plans accordingly. In considering the resources and information he wants to present, Jared thinks about the following:

- What **background** information is needed to ensure a common foundation? A good WebQuest scaffolds prior learning or common background knowledge into greater knowledge. Facts can be referred to, provided in a narrative, or made available through Web site links or a reading list.
- How can he make optimal use of **primary source documents**?
- Is there **enough** information available for **each role**?
- What sites would be meaningful for the **Group Synthesis** activity?
- **How long** does he want the class to spend on this topic and exercise?
- How should he **organize** the Process pages; for example,
  - What lists or links are long enough to warrant separate pages for readability and ease of use?

○ Are there separate Processes (phases) that should be shown separately, each with its own set of resources and other information?

○ What information makes best use of a narrative within the WebQuest vs. links to specific resources?

○ Where and how should links be placed so they aren't distracting?

> *Teacher note:* Using documentaries might be an effective way to establish a common knowledge base for your students. An example of one that might have been used for Anita's Religious Conflicts WebQuest in Chapter 5 is PBS's *Elusive Peace: Israel and the Arabs.* Links to video resources are in Other Resources: C in the back of this book.

One of the challenges in using WebQuests in a culturally diverse classroom is the assumption that all students have a common foundation of knowledge to respond to the specific WebQuest assignment. In reality, language barriers, cultural differences, varied socioeconomic backgrounds, and other differences influence students' perceptions and understanding of this "common foundation."

What particular challenges do you face in your classroom that require particular care in establishing a common knowledge base, validating understanding, and selecting resources for your WebQuests?

_____

_____

_____

Internet Resources

Search Engines

Numerous search engines, directories, and specialized search tools exist to help you find the specific resources you want your students to study. The textbox labeled Online Resources later in this chapter has an annotated list of search engines and other pertinent sites to assist you in refining your searches. Bernie Dodge has some tips about focusing searches to pinpoint sites to meet specific needs at http://webquest.sdsu.edu/searching/fournets .htm that you might want to review.

Selecting Web Sites

While many of the factors you need to consider in selecting appropriate Web resources for your students are the same as with any other type of material, some are unique to the online world. You want to select sites that are appropriate to the age and learning level of your students; are stable, reliable, and unbiased; and are easy to navigate. In some cases, you need to be concerned about Web accessibility issues (discussed briefly in Chapter 2 and in more detail later in this chapter). Web safety (covered in Chapter 6) is also a concern. YouTube, for example, might contain specific content fitting for your WebQuest, but as an unmanaged site, will also contain inappropriate videos. If you choose to include resources from such sites, you'll need to direct your students to the exact link and check to make sure your school's Internet filters will allow access to the material.

DO select sites that

- Contain primary source documents.
- Have other useful images, such as maps and illustrations.
- Provide a variety of learning tools, such as audio, interactivity, and multimedia.
- Are current.
- Are reliable. Check for government (.gov), education (.edu), or organization (.org) indicators and review the "About" page to determine the source or owner of the Web site.

DON'T select sites that

- Are geared toward adults.
- Contain numerous advertisements or commercial pop-ups (might suggest a lack of objectivity or educational purpose).
- Are difficult to navigate.
- Are hosted on free sites such as Geocities. (These sites tend to disappear or are not up-to-date.)

ADDITIONAL CAUTION is warranted for sites that

- Are unmanaged (such as YouTube, Wikipedia, etc.).

One favorite source of information for students is Wikipedia, the free, multilingual online encyclopedia created and edited by volunteers worldwide. A note of caution is in order, however; even if you are comfortable with the accuracy and objectivity of the content you use from this site, remember that it might change before your students access it. Because articles can be edited by anyone at any time, you'll need to recheck any selected resources for content changes during the WebQuest assignment period. Many teachers don't permit students to use Wikipedia as a resource because of inaccuracies and unreliability. Also, although resources are available in many languages, Wikipedia articles on the same topic differ in different languages because they aren't simply translated; the authors vary. (Note that Maria used Wikipedia for her Immigration WebQuest. Some of the factors she considered before citing it were the significant amount of information it contained, the accuracy and unbiased nature of the entry, and its readability at an eighth-grade level. And Ron used Wikipedia for his Geography WebQuest because of its clickable maps and other tools available within the topic.) However, many teachers won't use Wikipedia at all because they don't allow their students to use it as a source of information.

Links to some tools created by a few universities and organizations for evaluating Web sites are listed in the textbox labeled Online Resources near the end of this chapter. Those sites contain more detailed guidance for determining the reliability and objectivity of Internet pages.

The following sites might be helpful to you in finding online social studies materials, including primary source documents. Also, consult the specialized search engines and directories listed in the Online Resources textbox, as well as the social studies links cited in Chapter 5, or search "social studies" using one of the listed search engines.

Social Studies Links

Virtual Classrooms

- Virtual Social Studies Classroom—http://www.socialstudiesclassroom.com/
- Mr. Neal's Virtual Social Studies Classroom—http://www.virtualclassroom.net/main.htm
- Virtual Middle School Library (Social Studies Sites by Subject)—http://www.sldirectory.com/teachf/socsci.html
- Houghton Mifflin Social Studies (Links to Primary Sources)—http://www.eduplace.com/ss/hmss/primary.html

School and University Sites

- Indiana University (Social Studies Sources for K–12)—http://education.indiana.edu/~socialst/
- Radford University, Virginia (History and Social Studies Links)—http://www.radford.edu/~sbisset/history.htm

- California State University, Northridge (Lesson Plans and Internet Resources for Social Studies)—http://www.csun.edu/~hcedu013/index.html
- University of Texas (Maps)—http://www.lib.utexas.edu/maps/index.html
- University of OK College of Law (U.S. Historical Documents)—http://www.law.ou.edu/hist/
- Fordham University (Internet Modern History Sourcebook)—http://www.fordham.edu/halsall/mod/modsbook.html
- University of Houston (Digital History Online Textbook)—http://www.digitalhistory.uh.edu/
- Jefferson County Schools (Interactive Social Studies Sites by Grade Level)—http://jc-schools.net/tutorials/interactive.htm#Social%20Studies
- Nassau NY Board of Cooperative Education (Primary Source links)—http://www.kn.pacbell.com/wired/fil/pages/listdocumentpa.html
- Clarkston NY School District (Primary Source links)—http://www.ccsd.edu/link/LMS/Infolink/primarysource.htm
- Lawrence NY Public Schools (Primary Source links)—http://www.lawrence.org/edlinks/dbq/dbq.htm

State and Federal Resources

- State of California (Comprehensive, Searchable Social Studies Sites)—http://score.rims.k12.ca.us/
- Library of Congress (U.S. Legislation)—http://thomas.loc.gov/
- Library of Congress (American Memory)—http://memory.loc.gov/ammem/browse/
- U.S. Census Bureau (State and County Profiles)—http://quickfacts.census.gov/qfd/index.html
- U.S. Department of State (Country Information)—http://www.state.gov/countries/
- CIA World Factbook (Country Information)—https://www.cia.gov/cia/publications/factbook/index.html
- U.S. Army (Country Studies)—http://www.country-studies.com/

Media, Public Service, and Other

- BBC News (World Current Events)—http://news.bbc.co.uk/
- National Public Radio—http://www.npr.org/
- PBS—http://www.pbs.org/

- The History Channel (Speeches and Media)—http://www
  .history.com/media.do
- A&E Biographies—http://www.biography.com/search
- National Endowment for the Humanities ("EdSiteMent":
  Comprehensive Lesson Plans and Web Links)—http://
  edsitement.neh.gov/tab_lesson.asp?subjectArea=3
- Info Please (Country Information)—http://www.infoplease
  .com/countries.html
- Archiving Early America (Primary Source Documents)—http://
  www.earlyamerica.com/

Accessibility Issues

Web accessibility means the design methods, processes, and tools that allow those with disabilities (either physical or cognitive) to utilize the Internet at a target level and with a certain ease. The issues and efforts concerning accessibility are too numerous to discuss at length in this book, but some of your students are likely to have disabilities or language barriers you need to consider. You should perform accessibility tests while researching and selecting Web sites. One general tool for finding highly accessible Web sites is a new Google search engine, listed and explained in the Online Resources textbox near the end of this chapter. In Chapter 2, we listed two sites dealing with accessibility and Section 508 issues. One of the main attributes that makes a site fail 508 is the lack of text descriptions associated with images, because this is what a screen reader reads to a person with vision problems. Frames also need titles, or a text description of the function of that frame (example: a side panel may act as a menu bar).

Specific concerns you are likely to encounter, and tools you can use to test Web pages, are as follows:

- *Low or no vision.* A number of tests are available on the Web. One is Cynthia Says (http://www.cynthiasays.com/), which allows you to test how a site appears in a specific browser.
- *Color blindness.* Vischeck at http://www.vischeck.com/ simulates how a Web page you select would look based on the type of color blindness you input. Some of the page data or images might not be visible for those who have this condition.

> ● *Hearing impairment.* Sites with audio or video (without captioning or a transcript available) are a concern for those with hearing problems. If any students are hearing impaired, teachers need to choose sites with their needs in mind or provide alternative ways for those students to receive the information.
> ● *Flashing and seizures.* Certain flash rates and colors can trigger seizures in people with photosensitive epilepsy. Awareness of your students is key in selecting sites. Avoid sites that have pop-up ads or flashing special effects.
> ● *Reading level* (be sensitive to ESL students) can be assessed at http://juicystudio.com/services/readability.php.

Which of these accessibility issues need to be considered in your classroom?

_____

_____

_____

In Chapter 5, Anita was concerned about the language barrier some of her students face. Assess the three resources she used for the Roman Catholic Schism in Brazil for readability using Juicy Studio. Which of these resources would you keep and which would you eliminate? Are there alternate sites you can find that might be more suitable?

	Reading Level	Keep?	If Not, Alternate Site Recommended
1.			
2.			
3.			

Copyright, Fair Use, and Citation of Sources

Jared has noticed that many students seem confused about copyright laws and citing sources when they write reports or create multimedia presentations or Web sites. Most students (and many teachers as well) don't have a clear understanding of the concept of fair use. Copyright applies to all forms of media, including images, photographs, video, audio, and software. In certain circumstances, teachers and students may use portions of copyrighted material for educational purposes without obtaining permission from the copyright holder. Simply citing a source isn't a substitution for obtaining permission when it's required.

Jared's students like to use images and video clips in their PowerPoint presentations. Jared sees the benefits of using video in the classroom. Can he use a TV show he recorded at home? If he rents a movie, is it permissible to use it in his classroom? He wants to make certain he models ethical practices for his students and that they're aware of the laws. If, like Jared, you are confused about legal requirements, many good resources can be found on the Internet. A list of links to some of these resources on copyright, fair use, and citing sources is contained in the Online Resources textbox near the end of this chapter.

Other Resources

In additional to Internet resources, WebQuests might make use of books, newspapers, films, museum visits, plays, and any other learning media. Ask your school librarian to recommend a book that is germane to your topic or see Other Resources: C in the back of this book for links to lists of award-winning young adult novels and ones that are culturally significant. That listing also contains sites to help you find audio and video resources for your Process.

Exercises: Resources from Example WebQuests

Frank Parker listed two books as resources for the Zambia WebQuest in Chapter 3. What additional information about these resources might be helpful to students for them to complete the assignment efficiently?

_____

_____

_____

In Chapter 5 (Religious Conflicts WebQuest), the Process included several organizers to help students record their research results. Are these important or do they detract from higher-level learning?

_____

_____

_____

Are there similar (or different) tools that could be included in the Immigration assignment in Chapter 6 that would help clarify the Task or the Process, or help students think in different ways?

_____

_____

_____

Anita Bertz knew the Web sites she selected might be difficult for her students to comprehend entirely, so she compensated for this by creating language experts. Is this an acceptable approach? Are there other alternatives, or must all sites be at the appropriate comprehension level?

_____

_____

_____

In Chapter 7's WebQuest on Geography, no resources were assigned to individual roles; therefore, the Group Synthesis activity was based on a common set of data. What drawbacks do you see to this approach? How would you change this WebQuest (by assigning different roles or using different resources) to maximize the higher-level learning in the group activity? Be specific.

Drawbacks _____

_____

_____

_____

Revised Roles _____

_____

_____

_____

Individual Resource Suggestions _____

_____

_____

_____

Online Resources

This list of Web sites should be helpful to you in creating the WebQuest Process:

San Diego Unified School District

● WebQuest Process Tools—http://projects.edtech.sandi.net/
staffdev/tpss99/processguides/index.htm and http://projects
.edtech.sandi.net/staffdev/tpss99/processchecker.html

General Search Engines

● Google (standard version)—http://www.google.com/
● Google Scholar—http://scholar.google.com/
● Yahoo Search—http://www.yahoo.com/
● msn Search—http://www.msn.com/
● Ask.com—http://www.ask.com/

Meta Search Engines (search multiple engines at once)

● Dogpile—http://www.dogpile.com/
● Clusty—http://clusty.com/
● Mamma—http://mamma.com/
● Surfwax—http://surfwax.com/

Specialized Search Engines

● Allsearchengines.com (Lists search engines and searchable
  databases; e.g., Library links to searchable library databases
  throughout the world)—http://www.allsearchengines.com/
● Google Accessible Search (Identifies and prioritizes search
  results that are more easily usable by blind and visually
  impaired users)—http://labs.google.com/accessible/
● SDSU (List of Specialized Search Engines and Directories)—
  http://webquest.sdsu.edu/searching/specialized.html

Filtered Search Engines

● StopDog.com—http://www.stopdog.com/
● Ask for Kids—http://www.askforkids.com/
● KidsClick—http://www.kidsclick.org/
● Yahoo! Kids—http://kids.yahoo.com/

Evaluating Web Pages

● Duke University (See "Evaluating Information Sources"
  links)—http://library.duke.edu/services/instruction/
  libraryguide/
● Valdosta State University—http://www.valdosta.edu/library/
  learn/webevalcite.shtml
● Humboldt State University Library—http://library.humboldt
  .edu/owls/owl5-Web.htm
● University of Berkeley (Critical Evaluation of Resources and
  Tutorial)—http://www.lib.berkeley.edu/TeachingLib/Guides/
  Evaluation.html and http://www.lib.berkeley.edu/TeachingLib/
  Guides/Internet/Evaluate.html

Copyright, Fair Use, and Citation Resources

● The United States Copyright Office—http://www.copyright.gov/
● Copyright Web site—http://www.benedict.com/
● Copyright Kids—http://www.copyrightkids.org/
● Copyright Bay—http://www.stfrancis.edu/cid/copyrightbay/
● Resources from Hall Davidson (Scroll down to links to
  articles, charts, and quizzes)—http://www.halldavidson.net/
  downloads.html
● Modern Language Association (MLA)—http://www.mla.org/

EXAMPLE WEBQUEST NO. 5: VOTING RIGHTS AND RESPONSIBILITIES

Jared's lesson follows. In the next chapter, we'll look at finalizing the WebQuest design by writing Introductions and Conclusions. We'll also cover Web pages that aren't standard components, but are usually contained in a WebQuest.

WebQuest

Let Our Voices Be Heard!

▶ INTRODUCTION

In the United States, almost every adult citizen has the right to vote, although it took over two centuries to achieve this equity. Like our country, many other nations have faced the evolution of democracy. It was only in 2004 that Afghan women regained their right to vote; women and other classes (social, political, religious, ethnic, economic, etc.) still have little or no rights in many proclaimed democracies throughout the world.

How would you convince a government that excludes certain classes that all citizens have the right to vote? As a consultant for *Democracy for All*, a newly formed global organization focused on voting rights, you'll need to develop a solid strategy and formulate a compelling argument for your clients, certain classes of the country of Zawod. Your job is to analyze how change has been achieved in the past—both in the United States and recently in Afghanistan—and help the citizens of this newly developing democracy have their voices heard.

▶ TASK

Only certain groups can vote in the small country of Zawod. Government leaders there have been pressured by their trading partners and by certain worldwide organizations to expand voting rights to more Zawodians. A government insider (with far too liberal leanings if you ask President Jared!) has told *Democracy for All* that the Legislature might concede voting rights to one excluded group of Zawodians just to keep the pressure off. As a member of a consulting team representing one of four classes clamoring for the vote, you and your coworkers need to develop a short- and long-term strategy to convince the Legislature that the class you are representing should be the first one to gain voting status **(Task 1)**. Then, each team member will write a sixty-second TV ad **(Task 2)**. *Democracy for All* can afford to air only the best three ads on Zawod's two TV channels during the next Legislative session, so make sure your client's voice is heard!

▶ PROCESS

Background: All Teams

Country of Zawod

Zawod was formed ten years ago when it broke off from a larger country. A lack of infrastructure led the Legislature to enact certain convenient voting regulations, which the government believes have worked well. It encourages economic growth and the stability of family, and taxes don't have to be used to pay for expensive processes that would enable voting by smaller groups. In order to vote, a person must

- Be married, with at least one spouse having full-time employment.
- Speak the primary language, Jarzawese.
- Live within a two-hour walking distance of one of the five voting stations. About 80 percent of the population meets this criteria; most of the other 20 percent live in a plains area known as the Hinterlands.

U.S. Voting Rights

The entire class should already be familiar with the general history of U.S. voting rights, as well as the current voting requirements. If you want to refresh your knowledge, feel free to review the following:

U.S. Constitutional Provisions, including Amendments— http://www.usconstitution.net/

Current Voting Guidelines—http://www.abanet.org/publiced/ lawday/schools/lessons/handout_voting_guidelines.html

Scholastic Article: Three Contributors to U.S. Voting Rights— http://content.scholastic.com/browse/article.jsp?id=4638

Roles and Teams

Four groups from Zawod have approached your consulting firm *Democracy for All* and you'll be a member of one of the teams representing a client group. Teams will be assigned based on the alphabetical order of your last name (e.g., the first four students in alphabetical order will be assigned to Team I). The client groups each want the Legislature to enact measures that allow them to vote and also give them the tools they need to vote without undue hardship.

> *Team I* will represent the Zawodian Retirees Association (ZRA). Because most retirees don't have full-time jobs, they can't vote, even if they have voted in the past.
>
> *Team II* will represent the Hinterlands community.
>
> *Team III* will represent the Nozads. Members of this indigenous group live together in communities throughout the urban environments, working unskilled labor or selling native crafts. They have clung to their original culture and most speak only their native dialect.
>
> *Team IV* will represent the Young Zawodian Career Club. Members of this club are primarily single men and women. They are focused on building careers and have had neither the time nor inclination to marry and start families.

You'll play one of four research roles with a team. Each researcher studies a particular history to determine the best strategy to attain the right to vote; then, the team uses the combined knowledge to develop a plan. You'll decide which role you'll play within your team. The roles are

> U.S. Women's Suffrage Expert
>
> U.S. African American Suffrage Expert
>
> U.S. General Voting Rights History Expert
>
> Afghan Women's Suffrage Expert

Task 1. Your first homework assignment before the next class is to research the resources provided for your role. Then, your team will have two class periods to discuss and develop the short- and long-term strategies, timeline, and tactics that you'll recommend to your client group. Be sure to include anticipated responses to any objections the Legislature might have. For example, state how money will be raised if any funds must be spent to facilitate voting for your group, or explain why giving single people the vote won't contribute to the decline of the family unit. The plan should be at least four double-spaced typed pages and will be handed in at the beginning of the third class period and presented then or in the fourth class period. You'll have ten minutes to present and ten minutes to answer questions from your clients, represented by the other groups and President Jared. All team members must participate in the presentation.

Resources for Specific Consultant Roles

U.S. Women's Suffrage Movement History

Summary—http://www1.cuny.edu/portal_ur/content/voting_cal/women_suffrage.html

Digital History Textbook—http://www.digitalhistory.uh.edu/database/subtitles.cfm?titleID=39

U.S. African American Suffrage History

African American Odyssey—http://lcweb2.loc.gov/ammem/aaohtml/exhibit/aopart9.html

Introduction to Federal Voting Rights Laws—http://www.usdoj.gov/crt/voting/intro/intro.htm

The Voting Rights Act Discussion—http://www.oag.state.ny.us/family/kids/crime/voting.html

U.S. General Voting Rights History

History of U.S. Voting Rights (1790–present)—http://www.infoplease.com/timelines/voting.html

Chinese and Native American Voting Rights—http://www1.cuny.edu/portal_ur/content/voting_cal/americans_chinese.html

Puerto Rican Voting Rights—http://www1.cuny.edu/portal_ur/content/voting_cal/puerto_rican.html

Noncitizen Voting Rights—http://www.migrationinformation.org/USfocus/display.cfm?ID=265

Mexican American Voting Rights—http://www1.cuny.edu/portal_
ur/content/voting_cal/mexican_american.html

Primary Source Document: Voting Literacy Test—http://college
.hmco.com/history/us/resources/students/primary/voting.htm

Afghanistan Women's Suffrage

Afghanistan History Summaries:

BBC News—http://news.bbc.co.uk/2/hi/south_asia/
1569826.stm

InfoPlease—http://www.infoplease.com/ce6/world/
A0856490.html

Human Rights Watch—http://www.hrw.org/backgrounder/
asia/afghan-bck1023.htm

In 1992, the Taliban began taking power in Afghanistan and had control
of 90 percent of the country by 2000. See the PBS Article "Veiled in Fear"
at http://www.pbs.org/newshour/bb/asia/july-dec96/afghan_background_
10-9.html for a description of the treatment of women under the extremist
Islamic regime. The Taliban were defeated in August 2003.

Under current Afghanistan Electoral Law (adopted in 2004), all Afghan
citizens over the age of 18 who have not been deprived of political and civil
rights by an authoritative court and are registered to vote have the right to
vote. This law also forbids "direct or indirect restriction on voters and/or
candidates on the basis of language, ethnic, gender, tribal, geographic, religious, or social status."

See the following articles for narratives of Afghan women's continuing
fears during the new democratic elections:

Human Rights Watch Article: 2004 Elections—http://hrw.org/
campaigns/afghanistan/election2004.htm

Human Rights Watch Article: 2005 Elections—http://hrw.org/
backgrounder/wrd/afghanistan0805/index.htm

Task 2. Once all four plans have been presented, your homework assignment
(due the fifth class period) will be to write the sixty-second TV ad. If your
ad is one of the best three, it will premiere when you enact it (using your
teammates as cast members if you wish) after the judging is complete.

▶ EVALUATION

TASK 1: Develop a Strategy and Plan

Category	Exceeds Requirements	Meets Requirements	Partially Meets Requirements	Does Not Meet Requirements
Research 25%	Included research points from at least four sources and all four resource topics.	Included research points from at least four sources and all four resource topics.	Included research points from between two to four sources and two to four resource topics.	Included research points from less than two resource topics.
Collaboration 50%	The tactics and timeline supported the long-term strategy and creative solutions were proposed.	Most of the tactics and timeline supported the long-term strategy and creative solutions were proposed.	Some of the tactics and the timeline did not support the strategy and there was little creativity in proposed solutions.	The tactics, timeline, and strategy were not in sync; solutions were not creative or thoughtful.
Presentation 25%	Written presentation was logically organized and free of grammatical and typographical errors. The oral presentation was clear and all critical points were addressed. All questions were answered based on research.	Presentation was logically organized and free of grammatical and typographical errors (one to two errors). The oral presentation was clear and most of the critical points were addressed. Most questions were answered based on research.	Presentation was somewhat disorganized or contained more than five grammar and spelling mistakes. The oral presentation was not well organized or did not contain the most critical points. Several questions were not answered.	Presentation was poorly organized or contained more than ten grammar and spelling mistakes. The oral presentation was not well organized and did not contain the most critical points. Many questions were not answered.

TASK 2: Write a Sixty-Second TV Ad

Category	Exceeds Requirements	Meets Requirements	Partially Meets Requirements	Does Not Meet Requirements
General Writing Skills 50%	No spelling, grammar, or organizational mistakes.	One to two spelling, grammar, or organizational mistakes.	Three to four spelling, grammar, or organizational mistakes.	More than four spelling, grammar, or organizational mistakes.
Argument Supported by Facts 25%	At least three solid reasons support the ad argument.	At least two solid reasons support the ad argument.	At least one solid reason supports the ad argument.	No rationale for the ad argument.
Cohesiveness of Argument 25%	All rationale is consistent; no contradiction in the argument.	All rationale is consistent; one contradiction in the argument.	Rationale is somewhat inconsistent, more than one contradiction.	Rationale is inconsistent or facts are contradictory.

▶ CONCLUSION

At the end of this assignment, President Jared will announce whether the Legislature has been convinced to allow additional Zawodian group(s) to vote in the next election. Assuming your group gains this right, what civic responsibility do you think it has to itself and to the other groups who don't yet have the right to vote? We'll discuss this question as a class once the ads have premiered.

9 Finalizing Your WebQuest Design

This chapter draws on the five example WebQuests from the previous chapters as well as a new classroom scenario to examine the final additions to your WebQuest design: creating the Introduction, the Conclusion, a Teacher Page, and the Credits Page; using images and other tools; and assessing your product.

MEET POROMA KANYA . . .

I have a beautiful family, perfect parents and siblings really, a loving, supportive family in every way. But, growing up in Dhaka, Bangladesh, a big metropolitan city, I guess they had to be a bit strict as well. I had to be home before dark and things like that. And school was a family priority. In Bangladesh, there are schools that teach in Bangla, the native language, but I went to English medium schools where all the instruction is in English.

In the early grades, I was not a very good student. But, when I attended fourth grade in a fabulous school where I got lots of support from the teachers, I changed. I guess my transformation started with a silly little teenage book (I don't even remember the title or the author) about a little girl that was invisible, sort of like me. Her dad changed jobs and the family had to move. Instead of feeling bad, she took a chance to reinvent herself.

Since I was moving on to middle school, I saw an opportunity to reinvent myself as well. I started to gain more confidence and become more responsible for my own education. With the support of my family and teachers, I became a good student. One high school teacher in particular had a great influence on me. I could go to her for personal as well as academic advice. She and everyone in the school were approachable. I could go to the principal for a chat. I could even go to the chef with a request. I think it is a little different here in the United States, maybe not the same level of approachability. I am not sure why.

Janeka Gonzales teaches sociology in a large suburban high school in a town where most of the kids are privileged but probably don't consider themselves to be. Her classroom is fairly diverse ethnically, but less so racially and economically. Talking to Paroma, her student from Bangladesh, has given Janeka an idea about how to teach her lesson plan on the social impact of industrialization in a way that reaches outside the textbook discourses on topics such as the Industrial Revolution. She is particularly interested in having her students understand what personal and cultural factors affect government plans to industrialize and how the move away from an agrarian-dependent economy changes social conditions, class structures, population growth, and other sociological conditions.

Let's now look at the Introduction and Conclusion, the final two standard WebQuest components.

WEBQUEST INTRODUCTIONS

The Introduction is the first page of the WebQuest and is usually one to two paragraphs long. It introduces the lesson and should be compelling. A good introduction **tells** students about the assignment; a better introduction **appeals** to their interests; and the best introduction **pulls** them into the lesson by grabbing their attention and evoking their curiosity. Use words and images to which your particular student group relates and finds interesting. Create a mystery or suggest an adventure. Position the WebQuest as a competition.

Review the Introductions from the previous WebQuests and rate each attribute from 1 (good) to 3 (best).

After reading the Introduction, students will:	Zambia	Religious Conflicts	Immigration	Eastern European Geography	Voting Rights
Understand what topic they will be studying					
Have a general idea of how they will approach the lesson					
Believe the assignment will have relevance to them personally					
Feel the lesson is sensitive to their cultural background or special needs/ circumstances					
Want to click on the Task Page to see what's next					

What techniques used in the Introductions might be particularly effective for your classroom?

_____

_____

_____

Which might be least effective?

_____

_____

_____

What other tactics would work well in your classroom?

_____

_____

_____

Now, write a great Introduction for Janeka's WebQuest on Industrialization using Bangladesh's recent history as a backdrop for the lesson.

_____

_____

_____

_____

_____

_____

_____

_____

_____

WEBQUEST CONCLUSIONS

In addition to summarizing the lesson and the students' intended experience, the Conclusion should relate to the Introduction. A good conclusion also emphasizes, in some way, the higher-level learning process that has occurred (perhaps by revealing a surprising result of the assignment, the "hidden learning agenda" you hoped to achieve). The Conclusion might also be used to encourage additional study opportunities or to pose a set of follow-up questions to be discussed, so a scaffolding of knowledge continues. Whether the supplementary assignment is mandatory or optional, invite continued learning by employing the same type of "hooks" used in the Introduction (i.e., make further study compelling!).

Review the Conclusions from the previous WebQuests and rate each attribute from 1 (good) to 3 (best).

After reading the Conclusion, students will:	Zambia	Religious Conflicts	Immigration	Eastern European Geography	Voting Rights
Feel a sense of satisfaction for completing the assignment					
Gain an understanding of solid composition skills					
Be encouraged to continue their journey of discovery					
Feel the lesson related to them personally					

Now, based on the Introduction you wrote earlier, write a great Conclusion for Janeka's Industrialization WebQuest.

_____

_____

_____

_____

_____

_____

_____

_____

USING IMAGES AND OTHER TOOLS

Creating assignments on the computer allows you to integrate relevant images, documents, study tools, sound, video, animated icons, and educational games that can add to the appeal of the lesson, provide structure, and enhance the learning opportunity. Refer to the discussion in Chapter 8 for copyright and fair use issues and keep these in mind when you integrate images and other matter into your WebQuests. In the example WebQuests, some of the tools the teachers might have used are as follows.

Example No. 1: Zambia

- To demonstrate the excitement of WebQuest competition, have students race for "best times" in completing the Africa Puzzle Map found on School Net Namibia at http://www.schoolnet.na/games/map/africa.html.

Example No. 2: Religious Conflicts

- Insert symbols for the various religions on the Introduction page.
- Make the organizers and charts "clickable" word documents.
- Link a Zencast (a weekly transmission of Buddhist Dharma talks) or other religious podcast to the WebQuest; for a podcast directory, go to http://www.podcastdirectory.com/.

Example No. 3: Immigration

- Use a graphic organizer to guide the research; it's a good way to focus students who find research a particular challenge.
- Link to current news stories. Some places to look include http://www.choices.edu/resources/current.php and your local television and newspaper sites.
- Use other online video resources. Some might be
  - Interview Regarding Immigration and Poverty in Mexico (Google Video)
  - Lou Dobbs on Illegal Immigrants (YouTube)
  - Beyond the Border (PBS Films)

Example No. 4: Geography

- Insert relevant geography photographs (see conditions of use) into the WebQuest pages from the University of Berkeley site at http://geoimages.berkeley.edu/geoimages.html.

- Download political or satellite maps from Geology.com at http://geology.com/world/cameroon-satellite-image.shtml.
- Download or play (free) Eastern European music from Download.com at http://music.download.com/3605-8229_32-0.html.

Example No. 5: Voting Rights

- Create or download an image for each team to use as a consistent symbol for its team deliverables. For example, the symbol for the Zowads might be an icon of a craft (basket, doll, or clothing perhaps) and the image for the ZRA might be something associated with retirement. The respective image would then be incorporated in the team's strategic plan presentation and advertising campaign.

Which of these tools might be useful in the Industrialization WebQuest that Janeka Gonzales is writing?

_____

_____

_____

_____

_____

_____

TEACHER PAGE AND CREDITS

These pages present additional information referenced primarily by other teachers who might use the WebQuest. The Teachers Page(s) might include

- An *Introduction* in simple prose about what the lesson is designed to accomplish (different from the Introduction that is written to draw students to the lesson).
- Who the *Learners* are (grade level and subject; special considerations about accessibility requirements and cultural responsiveness might be articulated).

- *Standards* being addressed (could include NCSS, ISTE, specific state, and other applicable standards); see Other Resources: D for a mapping of standards to each of the example WebQuests in this book.
- A summary of the *Process* and any concerns (what areas might be easy and those that might be difficult, requiring assistance).
- *Resource* listing and links.

In QuestGarden, the above pages are stored separately from the Student Pages and accessed by clicking on Teacher's Page in the template.

The Credits Page (included in the Student Pages section) might include

- Reference to certain resources, such as downloaded images, where a citation is required for use.
- An acknowledgement of other lessons, WebQuests, etc., that were used or consulted and created by others.
- A thank-you to others who contributed to creating the WebQuest.
- Permission for others to use or adapt the new WebQuest.

ASSESSING YOUR WEBQUEST

As mentioned in Chapter 4, you should use Tom March's WebQuest assessment tool at http://bestwebquests.com/bwq/matrix.asp to rate the attributes of your finished product. First, however, review the following seven points adapted from his "red flags" list (2007a).

Tom March's Seven Points for a Great WebQuest

- There should be no right answer; students must engage in critical thinking and form opinions.
- Information should not be merely gathered, but used as a basis for additional learning.
- There needs to be criteria against which students formulate their end product (creativity is great, but it should not be "anything goes").
- A group process should exist so that individual knowledge is synthesized.
- Everyone must participate (role work should be balanced).
- The lesson being studied should be connected to today's global issues ("Rich, Real, and Relevant").
- After a struggle, learning is transformative.

Select one of the example WebQuests and assess it against these seven points, jotting your appraisal next to each bullet point on the previous page. Are there areas that fail? If so, what changes can be made so that it is transformed into a great WebQuest?

Now that you have studied all aspects of WebQuests in the context of being a culturally responsive educator, the next chapter will provide you with some additional thoughts about humanistic education, as well as the opportunity to apply the WebQuest concepts holistically in your own classroom environment.

10 The Challenge Ahead

A Quest for Peace

Your curriculum might be jam-packed with curricular requirements, and the pressure to adopt new districtwide instructional models is perhaps intense. We are well aware of the challenges facing today's teachers. Indeed, proscribed curricula, increasing reliance on high-stakes testing, and restrictive mandates such as those of the Elementary and Secondary Education Act (NCLB) can potentially limit the practical use of WebQuests. Despite these limitations, however, we know that you are thinking about the ideas in this book and that you are particularly sensitive to the notion of building unity in your classroom. Maybe you have already strategized ways to implement WebQuests within the contexts of the social sciences and the ideal of cultural responsiveness.

Remember, though, that these are *ideas*. And as teachers, as reflective practitioners, you are critical to how these ideas will take shape in the classroom. What you think and what you do matters. How you respond to your students—how you implement WebQuests—is limited only by your intentionality, your imagination, and *your* ideas. Indeed, ideas start with people, or as David Hansen (2007) notes, ". . . ideas take form through the initiative of individual persons who seek to respond to particular concerns, problems, fears, and hopes" (p. 1).

So, what do you hope to accomplish? How might you enrich the lives of your students by more culturally responsive teaching and learning? How might the WebQuest approach foster dialogue, critical thinking, and problem solving?

What is your action plan? Jot down your ideas below.

_____

_____

_____

_____

_____

_____

HUMANISTIC EDUCATION

As you move forward with your plan to use the WebQuest approach to activate cultural responsiveness in teaching and learning, we would like you to consider an even broader perspective to refine and extend your ideas: humanistic education. In our view, humanistic education in theory and practice is dedicated to the development of human happiness and its connection to good societies. According to Tsunesaburo Makiguchi (2002), "education is the key factor influencing the destiny of a society. It is education which supplies talents and abilities to all other fields, and it is education which can nurture good character, ethical behavior, and social consciousness within the members of a society" (p. 190). We can assume that humanistic education begins with a community of learners, a place where

- Teachers and learners view each other as human beings living together in an *interconnected and interdependent world.*
- Learning is the result of *direct experience supported* by curriculum resources.
- Learning is not imposed but *elicited* from each learner's experience, interests, and questions.
- Learners are *guided* by teachers, parents, and other adults. (Adapted from Dayle Bethel's introduction to Makiguchi's *Geography of Human Life,* p. xix.)

In this post-9/11 world, challenges to global awareness and world peace may seem insurmountable, especially given day-to-day classroom worries. But we believe the classroom is precisely where educating for tolerance and global citizenship—and where local unity and subsequently where world unity—begins. How are your students faring?

Your school district likely has a social studies or citizenship education curriculum that begins to address these issues, but is the current curriculum adequate for such an undertaking? Is the instruction adequate? Not sure? The following binaries adapted from Gloria Ladson-Billings' (2005) essay *Differing Concepts of Citizenship* might help you to get a critical sense of the inadequacies of some curriculum and instruction (Ladson-Billings, 2005, pp. 70–72). Where is emphasis placed in your school? Circle your hunches.

Rote-memorization of facts	or	Emerging facts from meaningful and authentic contexts
Textbook-determined content	or	Content linked to students' life experiences
Focus on compliance with laws	or	Focus on expressions of guaranteed freedoms
Passive teaching and learning	or	Active teaching and learning
Avoidance of controversial issues	or	Debating controversial issues
Teacher-controlled discourse	or	Encouragement of independent thinking
Low-track curriculum for some	or	High-quality curriculum for all
Focus on a national agenda	or	Focus on global issues
Standardized testing	or	Authentic assessment

Circles in the left column are problematic, especially if your intention is to increase participatory democracy. As Gloria Ladson-Billings (2005) asserts, "the paradox of attempting to use passive, irrelevant, noncontroversial curriculum and instruction to prepare students for active citizenship in a multicultural society is startling" (p. 72).

So, how can active, global citizenship be cultivated? Well, in many ways, by virtue of considering the ideas in this book, you have already begun. To extend these ideas, however, the work of the Boston Research Center for the 21st Century (BRC) might provide a useful philosophical compass to help us find our way. The BRC is dedicated to fostering a worldwide discourse of peace and understanding through the "active cultivation of an inclusive sense of community, locally and globally." The foundation of this cultivation rests upon three values:

- "*Wisdom* to perceive the interconnectedness of all life;
- *Courage* not to fear but to respect differences and strive to learn from people of all cultures; and
- *Compassion* that extends beyond the near and familiar to all those suffering far away" (Noddings, 2005, p. v.).

Might these ideals provide the philosophical underpinning for the practice of cultivating peace in your social studies classroom? What are the possibilities? What do you think?

_____

_____

_____

But how can these ideals manifest themselves in the classroom? As you explore the possibilities of your own ideas for action, review three promising and powerful curriculum and instruction models that secondary teachers already use in their classrooms. As you read the brief descriptions and explore the Web sites discussed below, think about how WebQuests might be integrated into these approaches.

The Choices Program

Developed for educators by the Thomas I. Watson Institute for International Studies at Brown University, this program seeks to expand public discourse and informed decision making into secondary classrooms through student examination of historical and global issues. As its title suggests, this model relies upon the notion of *choice*. You present students with competing visions of the future and then ask your students to select one vision to research and defend. For example, one of the units of study, *U.S. Role in the World: Four Futures,* prompts students to make a judgment regarding the level of U.S. engagement around the world. As you can imagine, the discussions can be lively as students debate the validity of their classmates' thinking as competing interpretations clash. With your facilitation, however, common ground and an understanding of multiple perspectives can be promoted. (See http://www.choices.edu/.)

Workable Peace

Another imaginative model, Workable Peace, developed by the Consensus Building Institute, is designed to "enliven moral reasoning" and build "social and civic skills" through the integration of conflict resolution into the secondary curriculum. (See http://www.workablepeace.org.) Stacie Nicole Smith and David Fairman (2005) provide an overview of the model, the challenges of integrating conflict management, and the differences this strategy might make on entrenched attitudes and behaviors. Similar to the Choices Program, Workable Peace attempts to teach "conflict analysis and management in the context of historical and current events" (Smith & Fairman, 2005, p. 44). Smith and Fairman describe Ms. Gearhy's tenth-grade world history class and how her students expressed their responses to terrorism following the events of September 11. Again, students responded to four perspectives and prepared for a discourse by mapping their "interests, beliefs, emotions, and identities" (p. 40).

Freedom Writers

The Freedom Writers model grew out of the experiences of Erin Gruwell and her students at Woodrow Wilson High School in Long Beach, California. Ms. Gruwell struggled to find relevance and to promote tolerance, understanding, and unity for her diverse students who were openly hostile to those outside their racial or ethnic group. Her diary reveals how she came upon a strategy to "reach and empower" her students through the universal teacher duty of intercepting a hurtful note passed between students. What transpired was the beginning of a revealing and emotional discovery of her students' lives through their journal entries. But the students also discovered much about themselves, as well as the lives of Anne Frank and other victims of the Holocaust. (See www.freedomwritersfoundation.org.)

Each of these models, in combination with the ideas of cultural responsiveness, humanistic education, and WebQuesting, have great potential to help to make your classes more relevant to the emerging, active, global citizens in your charge. Sometimes, as teachers, we lose sight of what is most important: the development and happiness of each student. We hope the ideas presented in this book resonate with you and with your students.

A FINAL QUEST

We would like to leave you with one final and very challenging task: synthesize what you have learned by constructing a "Quest for Peace" using your students and your curriculum. Refer back to the ideas you brainstormed in the previous chapters and expand upon them here to use as notes for building your assignment.

Who are your students? What are their stories? How do they learn best? What is your vision for them? What is their vision? Are there physical, cognitive, or language challenges for you to consider?

_____

_____

_____

_____

_____

_____

_____

_____

_____

_____

What lesson plan do you want to teach? How will it inspire and transform your students? Will they feel a personal connection to the topic or theme? How long do you want to devote to the lesson?

_____

_____

_____

What tasks might engage them? Does the assignment encourage complex thinking and higher-level problem solving? Can competing viewpoints be used effectively?

_____

_____

_____

What dimensions of the final project do you want to assess?

_____

_____

_____

What technology resources or other tools can you use to make the lesson more efficient or to help students organize their work?

_____

_____

_____

What other resources are available and appropriate (Internet sites, video, audio, books, etc.)? Do they meet the appropriate accessibility, readability, and other tests you have determined are necessary to perform?

_____

_____

_____

_____

_____

_____

What are possible roles? Can work be distributed fairly? How many teams will result? Is the amount of output manageable?

_____

_____

_____

_____

_____

_____

Now that you have thought through some of the key considerations and are ready to begin creating your WebQuest, log on to QuestGarden or build the assignment on your own Web pages or with one of the other tools previously discussed.

KEEPING THE QUEST ALIVE

Don't let your journey end with a final WebQuest. Take a few minutes to write down ten more ideas you have for using this technology in a culturally sensitive way in your classroom over the next few years. Your ideas may be about themes, topics, technology, cultures, situations . . . anything that will encourage complex thinking, help connect students' personal narratives to the larger social narrative, and prepare your students to make good decisions as global citizens.

1. _____

_____

2. _____

_____

3. _____

_____

4. _____

   _____

5. _____

   _____

6. _____

   _____

7. _____

   _____

8. _____

   _____

9. _____

   _____

10. _____

    _____

Other Resources

A. TEN THEMATIC STRANDS IN SOCIAL STUDIES

    I. Culture
    II. Time, Continuity, and Change
    III. People, Places, and Environments
    IV. Individual Development and Identity
    V. Individuals, Groups, and Institutions
    VI. Power, Authority, and Governance
    VII. Production, Distribution, and Consumption
    VIII. Science, Technology, and Society
    IX. Global Connections
    X. Civic Ideals and Practices

B. NATIONAL EDUCATIONAL TECHNOLOGY STANDARDS FOR STUDENTS

1. Creativity and Innovation

Students demonstrate creative thinking, construct knowledge, and develop innovative products and processes using technology. Students:

    a. apply existing knowledge to generate new ideas, products, or processes.
    b. create original works as a means of personal or group expression.
    c. use models and simulations to explore complex systems and issues.
    d. identify trends and forecast possibilities.

2. Communication and Collaboration

Students use digital media and environments to communicate and work collaboratively, including at a distance, to support individual learning and contribute to the learning of others. Students:

    a. interact, collaborate, and publish with peers, experts or others employing a variety of digital environments and media.
    b. communicate information and ideas effectively to multiple audiences using a variety of media and formats.
    c. develop cultural understanding and global awareness by engaging with learners of other cultures.
    d. contribute to project teams to produce original works or solve problems.

3. Research and Information Fluency

Students apply digital tools to gather, evaluate, and use information. Students:

  a. plan strategies to guide inquiry.

  b. locate, organize, analyze, evaluate, synthesize, and ethically use information from a variety of sources and media.

  c. evaluate and select information sources and digital tools based on the appropriateness to specific tasks.

  d. process data and report results.

4. Critical Thinking, Problem Solving, & Decision Making

Students use critical thinking skills to plan and conduct research, manage projects, solve problems and make informed decisions using appropriate digital tools and resources. Students:

  a. identify and define authentic problems and significant questions for investigation.

  b. plan and manage activities to develop a solution or complete a project.

  c. collect and analyze data to identify solutions and/or make informed decisions.

  d. use multiple processes and diverse perspectives to explore alternative solutions.

5. Digital Citizenship

Students understand human, cultural, and societal issues related to technology and practice legal and ethical behavior. Students:

  a. advocate and practice safe, legal, and responsible use of information and technology.

  b. exhibit a positive attitude toward using technology that supports collaboration, learning, and productivity.

  c. demonstrate personal responsibility for lifelong learning.

  d. exhibit leadership for digital citizenship.

6. Technology Operations and Concepts

Students demonstrate a sound understanding of technology concepts, systems, and operations. Students:

  a. understand and use technology systems.

  b. select and use applications effectively and productively.

  c. troubleshoot systems and applications.

  d. transfer current knowledge to learning of new technologies.

C. SITES FOR SELECTING SPECIALIZED RESOURCES

Young Adult Books

Consult your YA or school librarian, or review the lists on these sites:

Young Adult Library Services Association (YALSA)

- Best Books for Young Adults—http://www.ala.org/ala/yalsa/ booklistsawards/bestbooksya/bestbooksyoung.htm

Boston Public Library

- Booklists for Teens—http://www.bpl.org/teens/booklists/index.htm

Madison, WI Public Library

- Multicultural Fiction for Teens—http://www.madisonpubliclibrary .org/youth/booklists/multicultural_teens.html

The Public Library of Cincinnati and Hamilton County, OH

- Race in America (Books for Older Teens)—http://teenspace .cincinnatilibrary.org/books/booklist.asp?id=teenrace

Salt Lake County Library Services, UT

- Latino Literature for Children and Young Adults— http://www.slco.lib.ut.us/booklists/latino_literature.pdf

Stanly County Public Library, NC

- Asian and Asian-American Cultures Reading List (Ages 12 and Up)—http://www.stanlylib.org/kidlit_multicultural.html

National Council for the Social Studies

- Notable Trade Books for Young People— http://www.socialstudies.org/resources/notable/

Video Resources

Search your Video rental store or site, or scan the following:

Discovery Education Streaming

- http://streaming.discoveryeducation.com/index.cfm

PBS Video Store

- American Experience—http://www.shoppbs.org/family/ index.jsp?categoryId=1412580
- Hands-On History—http://www.shoppbs.org/family/ index.jsp?categoryId=1412581

Search Engines (Video)

- AltaVista Video Internet Search—http://www.altavista.com/video/
- Yahoo Video Search—http://video.search.yahoo.com/
- Google Video Search—http://video.google.com/

Audio Resources

Search Engines (Audio)

- AltaVista Audio Internet Search—http://www.altavista.com/audio/
- Yahoo Audio Search—http://audio.search.yahoo.com/

London South Bank University

- Museophile: Virtual Audio Library—http://archive.museophile.org/
  audio/

D. STANDARDS ASSOCIATED
WITH EXAMPLE WEBQUESTS

Example No. 1: One Zambia, One Nation?
NCSS Thematic Strands: I, III, VI
NETS-S: 1.a, 1.d, 2.a, 2.d, 3.a, 3.b, 3.d, 4.a, 4.b, 4.c, 5.a, 6.a, 6.b

Example No. 2: Religious Conflict: Is an End in Sight?
NCSS Thematic Strands: I, III, IV, V
NETS-S: 1.a, 1.d, 2.a, 2.d, 3.b, 3.d, 4.a, 4.d, 5.a, 6.a, 6.b

Example No. 3: Lights, Camera, Action! An Immigration Perspective
NCSS Thematic Strands: I, II, III, V, VI
NETS-S: 1.a, 1.b, 1.c, 2.a, 2.b, 2.d, 3.b, 3.d, 4.a, 4.b, 4.c, 4.d, 5.a, 6.a, 6.b

Example No. 4: Calling All Cartographers!
NCSS Thematic Strands: III, V, VII, VIII, IX
NETS-S: 1.a, 1.b, 1.d, 2.a, 2.b, 2.d, 3.b, 3.c, 3.d, 4.a, 4.b, 4.c, 4.d, 5.a, 6.a, 6.b
NGS: 1, 3, 7, 11, 15, 18

Example No. 5: Let Our Voices Be Heard!
NCSS Thematic Strands: I, II, III, IV, V, VI, X
NETS-S: 1.a, 1.b, 1.d, 2.a, 2.d, 3.a, 3.b, 3.c, 3.d, 4.a, 4.b, 4.c, 4.d, 5.a, 6.a, 6.b

References

Banks, J. A., & Banks, C. A. (2001). *Multicultural education: Issues and perspectives* (4th ed.). Boston: Allyn & Bacon.

Barton, K. C., & Levstik, L. S. (2004). *Teaching history for the common good.* Mahwah, NJ: Lawrence Erlbaum Associates.

The Choices Program. (2007). Retrieved July 17, 2007, from http://www.choices.edu

Cotton, K. (2003). Principals and student achievement: what the research says. Alexandria, VA: Association for Supervision and Curriculum Development.

Denzin, N. K., & Lincoln, Y. S. (Eds.). (2000). *Handbook of qualitative research* (2nd ed.). Thousand Oaks, CA: Sage.

Dodge, B. (1995, February). *Some thoughts about WebQuests.* Retrieved May 15, 2007, from http://webquest.sdsu.edu/about_webquests.html

Dodge, B. (2005, March 23). WebQuest vs. Kleenex. *WebQuest News.* Retrieved May 15, 2007, from http://webquest.org/news/index.html

Freedom Writers Foundation. (2006). *Freedom Writers Foundation.* Retrieved July 17, 2007, from http://www.freedomwritersfoundation.org

Gay, G. (2000). *Culturally responsive teaching: Theory, research and practice.* New York: Teachers College Press.

Hansen, D. (2007). (Ed.). *Ethical visions: Philosophies in practice.* New York: Teachers College Press.

International Society for Technology in Education. (2007). *National education technology standards for students.* Eugene, OR: Author.

Ladson-Billings, G. (2001). *Crossing over to Canaan: The journey of new teachers in diverse classrooms.* San Francisco: Jossey-Bass.

Ladson-Billings, G. (2005). Differing concepts of citizenship: Schools and communities as sites of civic development. In N. Noddings (Ed.), *Educating citizens for global awareness* (pp. 69–80). New York: Teachers College Press.

Makiguchi, T. (2002). The functions of society. In D. Bethel (Ed.), *Geography of human life* (pp. 187–198). San Francisco: Caddo Gap Press.

March, T. (2007a). The seven red flags: Warning signs when sifting WebQuests. *BestWebQuests. com.* Retrieved May 12, 2007, from http://bestwebquests.com/tips/red_flags.asp

March, T. (2007b). Criteria for assessing best WebQuests. *BestWebQuests.com.* Retrieved May 12, 2007, from http://bestwebquests.com/bwq/matrix.asp

March, T. (2007c). About best WebQuests. *BestWebQuests.com.* Retrieved May 12, 2007, from http://bestwebquests.com/about/default.asp

National Council for the Social Studies. (1992). *A vision of powerful teaching and learning in the social studies: Building social understanding and civic efficacy.* Retrieved April 11, 2007, from http://www.socialstudies.org/positions/powerful

Nieto, S. (1999). *The light in their eyes: Creating multicultural learning communities.* New York: Teachers College Press.

Nieto, S. (2000). *Affirming diversity: The sociopolitical context of multicultural education.* Reading, MA: Addison Wesley Longman.

Noddings, N. (2005). (Ed.). *Educating citizens for global awareness.* New York: Teachers College Press.

Smith, S. N., & Fairman, D. (2005). The integration of conflict resolution into the high school curriculum: The example of workable peace. In N. Noddings (Ed.), *Educating citizens for global awareness* (pp. 40–56). New York: Teachers College Press.

U.S. Department of Education National Center for Education Statistics. (2006). *Fast facts.* Retrieved July 16, 2007, from http://nces.ed.gov/fastfacts/display.asp?id=96

U.S. Department of Education National Center for Education Statistics. (2007a). *Language minority school-age children.* Retrieved July 16, 2007, from http://nces.ed.gov/programs/coe/2007/section1/indicator06.asp

U.S. Department of Education National Center for Education Statistics. (2007b). *Racial/ethnic distribution of public school students.* Retrieved July 16, 2007, from http://nces.ed.gov/programs/coe/2007/section1/indicator05.asp

Villegas, A., & Lucas, T. (2002). *Educating culturally responsive teachers.* Albany: State University of New York Press.

Workable Peace. (2007). *Workable peace.* Retrieved July 17, 2007, from www.workablepeace.org

Suggested Readings

Cultural Responsiveness in the Classroom

In addition to the books and articles cited in References, the following are suggested readings for cultural issues and responsiveness in the classroom:

Banks, J. A. (1999). *An introduction to multicultural education.* Needham Heights, MA: Allyn & Bacon.

Banks, J. A. (Ed.). (2003). *Diversity and citizenship education: Global perspectives.* San Francisco: Jossey-Bass.

Baruth, L. G., & Manning, M. L. (1992). *Multicultural education: Theory and practice.* Boston: Allyn & Bacon.

Cushman, K. (2003). *Human diversity in action: Developing multicultural competencies for the classroom* (2nd ed.) Boston: McGraw Hill.

Darling-Hammond, L. (Ed.). (2002). *Learning to teach for social justice.* New York: Teachers College Press.

Delpit, L. (1995). *Other people's children: Cultural conflict in the classroom.* New York: New Press.

Delpit, L., & Dowdy, J. K. (Eds.). (2002). *The skin that we speak: Thoughts on language and culture in the classroom.* New York: New Press.

Echevarria, J., Vogt, M. E., & Short, D. J. (2000). *Making content comprehensible for English language learners.* Boston: Allyn & Bacon.

Fine, M. (2003). *Silenced voices and extraordinary conversations: Re-imagining schools.* New York: Teachers College Press.

Gollnick, D., & Chin, P. C. (2002). *Multicultural education in a pluralistic society* (6th ed.) New York: Prentice Hall.

Hernandez, H. (1997). *Teaching in multilingual classrooms: A teacher's guide to context, process, and content.* Upper Saddle River, NJ: Prentice Hall.

Klein, M. D., & Chen, D. (2001). *Working with children from culturally diverse backgrounds.* Toronto, Ontario, Canada: Thomson.

Kohn, A. (1999). *The schools our children deserve.* New York: Houghton Mifflin.

Kozol, J. (1991). *Savage inequalities.* New York: Crown Publishers.

Krashen, S. D., & Terrell, T. D. (1983). *The natural approach: Language acquisition in the classroom.* Englewood Cliffs, NJ: Alemany.

Levine, E. (1993). *Freedom's children: Young civil rights activists tell their own stories.* New York: Puffin.

Martin, J. R. (2002). *Cultural miseducation: In search of a democratic solution.* New York: Teachers College Press.

Moses, M. S. (2002). *Embracing race.* New York: Teachers College Press.

Sleeter, C. E. (1996). *Multicultural education as social activism.* Albany: State University of New York Press.

Sleeter, C. E. (2001). *Culture, difference, and power.* New York: Teachers College Press.

Spring, J. (2003). *Deculturalization and the struggle for equality: A brief history of the education of dominated cultures in the United States* (4th ed.). New York: McGraw-Hill.

Takaki, R. (1993). *In a different mirror: A history of multicultural America.* New York: Little Brown.

Index